Close-Up

Close-Up

Up

How to Read the American City

Grady Clay

The University of Chicago Press
Chicago and London

The University of Chicago Press, Chicago 60637
The University of Chicago Press, ltd., London

©1973, 1980 by Grady Clay
All rights reserved. Published 1973
Phoenix edition 1980
Printed in the United States of America

84   5 4

ISBN: 0-226-10945-3
LCN: 79-26307

Contents

I have long nourished a fascination for what is *not* there, for the hidden and the partially revealed, and it was in pursuit of this elusive environmental quality that I wrote the hardback edition of *Close-Up*. Hardly was that first edition off the press when I had the first sweet-and-sour reactions: "Yes, but why didn't I have an answer? Yes, but why didn't I go further and offer prescriptions and programs?" All this in spite of my determined and no doubt obstinate refusal to do so in *Close-Up*. For it was clear to me in late 1972 when I was finishing the book that the world of print and electronic media was already crammed with instant solutions to the so-called urban crisis of the moment. I did not want to be drawn into that overcrowded racket. And it was equally clear, at least to me, that all too few of the instant soothsayers and necromancers possessed either a key to the future or a prescription for the present that might survive a single harsh test.

Such a test came more quickly than I had expected, for hardly was the first edition of this book in circulation when the Arabian oil embargo of 1973 suddenly made my comments at the end of the fifth chapter and throughout the last chapter more germane and apt than even the most bloody-minded author could have wished. Subsequent events—including long lines of "me-first" motorists at the gasoline pumps in 1979—make it possible for me now to remain content with what I wrote seven years earlier, that "this nation was not chosen by God in his wisdom to be eternally the most wealthy, wise and energetic among all nations of the earth. It must learn a different game, plan with a smaller set of chips." I also predicted that "as energy grows more expensive—gasoline at $2 per gallon, for example—we will reconsider our every move and mode."

Preface

Such realism remains for me the basic equipment with which to begin every examination of the American and other cities now engaged in conurbation. All cities continue to change, in response to access to and control over their energy supplies, as well as to their will to exploit and conserve.

But our ability to penetrate our surroundings—to distinguish myth from reality, wish from fulfillment—has only begun to cope with environmental change. With the added sophistication of television and computers, it becomes even more tempting for us to cope by staying indoors, glued to the expanding cornucopia of one-dimensional learning, and to neglect further the hard evidence which lurks all around us outside the walls. The new books and studies coming from landscape analysts suggest improved ways of looking, new tools for cutting through the first curtain separating us from environmental reality. I am happy to acknowledge that some of those specialists found *Close-Up* to be useful, and I hope that all readers of this newest edition will have the same rewards.

Grady Clay
Louisville, Kentucky
September 12, 1979

Observations such as these are as much reflection as invention; they are the bounce-back from many exchanges with friends, colleagues, and strangers, as well as with environments. Those who have contributed in any way to all this are, of course, absolved from any responsibility for errors of commission or omission.

Notable among the contributors is Charles William Brubaker whose sharp eye, perceptive mind, and quick hand have captured many a complex environment, and whose generous collaboration on this book is deeply appreciated. I am especially indebted to Professor Albert Fein whose urgings prompted me to put these ideas, some of them scattered in early form through lectures and articles, into book form, and whose advice as Consulting Editor on this book has been invaluable.

I should acknowledge a special debt to R. Whitney Ellsworth and Peter Davison who, long ago, encouraged me to translate these ideas into print.

Not all journalists have enjoyed such freedom to look, investigate, and write as was mine during productive years on *The Louisville Courier-Journal*. My thanks go to Mark Ethridge, Barry Bingham, Sr., and Cary Robertson, then Sunday Editor, who maintained for many of us a level of professional freedom all too scarce in daily journalism.

This book owes special acknowledgment to the insights and advice of my wife, Nanine H. Clay; and to many inputs over the years from city-watching associates and friends who include: Donald Appleyard, Brian Berry, Frank L. Elmer, Carl Feiss, Brian R. Goodey, John Griffalconi, Lawrence Halprin, Charles W. Harris, Jr., Edward Higbee, Basil Honikman, Patrick Horsbrugh, John Brinckerhoff Jackson, Jane Jacobs, Philip Lewis, Jr., Ron Lovinger, Kevin Lynch, Ian McHarg, Martin Meyerson, Douglas Nunn, Harvey Perloff, Larry Peterson, Art Seidenbaum, Paul Spreiregen, Philip Thiel, William Warntz, William L. C. Wheaton, and William L. Whyte, Jr.

I owe a special debt to many readers of *Landscape Architecture Quarterly* for their lively exchanges of views on the changing scene; and to Jem Roberts and Elizabeth R. Lyon for their research on the history of Piedmont Road, Atlanta, and its strips.

An early formulation of some of these ideas was made possible in 1967 by the energetic explorations of graduate students at Northwestern University's Medill

Acknowledgments

School of Journalism. As a team, led by David Sibbet, they produced a "Recognition Manual for Chicago," and included: Barbara Amazaki, Sue Golden Berg, Gary Braasch, Dick Chady, Carolyn Erlicher, Carole Etzler, Dennis Fisher, Tom Girard, Al Jaklich, David Jones, Jim Kaplan, Ed Kimbrell, Judy Kraines, Phil Landrum, Marti Lane, Andrew H. Malcolm, Nancy Middlestead, Dave Richert, Neil Rosenberg, Sue Salzar, Stu Schwartz, Grid Toland, Comini Torrevilles, John Walker, Peter Werner, Mike Whitney, and Esther Zimmerer.

For specific assistance as local guides and/or suppliers of information and insight into many localities, I am indebted to: Daniel M. H. Hickey—Albany, New York; Mr. and Mrs. Lawson P. Calhoun and Boisfevilliet Jones—Atlanta, Georgia; Delt Johnson—Auburn, Indiana; Bill Lamont—Boulder, Colorado; Mr. and Mrs. James C. Rouse—Columbia, Maryland; Charles W. Eliot and John Ross West—Columbus, Indiana; Grady Clay III, Mrs. Edward Hilliard, Jr., and Robert Rohe—Denver, Colorado; Carl Carbone, Mr. and Mrs. John Wyper, and Mrs. Ellsworth Grant—Hartford, Connecticut; Mr. and Mrs. Robert Adams—Hays, Kansas; Mrs. Helen Bird, Robert R. Feagin, Marvin Hill, Richard E. Johnston, George Wachendorf, Claude T. Yates—Jacksonville, Florida; Charles Munson—Kansas City, Missouri; Mr. and Mrs. Calvin Hamilton, Dean and Mrs. Samuel Hurst, Dean and Mrs. Harvey Perloff, and Art Seidenbaum— Los Angeles, California; Ward Dennis, John Holley, Craig Lindelow, John J. McKay, Jr., Flew Murphy, and Mr. and Mrs. English Solomon—Macon, Georgia; Professor and Mrs. Philip Lewis, Jr. and Professor and Mrs. Bruce Murray— Madison, Wisconsin; Professor and Mrs. F. Gene Ernst—Manhattan, Kansas; William Manly, William Rock, and Jim Schwartz—Milwaukee, Wisconsin; Julius Gy. Fabos, Ron Lovinger, Robert Riley, and Irvin Zube—Oregon; John Perry, Paul Pintarich, William G. Proctor, Andy Rocchia, Eugene M. Snyder, and John Storrs—Portland, Oregon; Dieter Hammerschlag and Edward Higbee—Rhode Island; O. K. Armstrong—Savannah, Georgia; George McCue—St. Louis, Missouri; Ewing H. Miller and Richard C. Tuttle—Terre Haute, Indiana.

Many persons have reacted thoughtfully to early versions of this book, and I am especially indebted to: Charles William Brubaker, Frank Elmer, Gil Jordan, Robert M. Leary, Mildred Lensing, Eldridge Lovelace, David W. Maurer, Dana Munro, Dr. William McGlothlin, John Osman, Larry Peterson, Don Ridings, Joan Riehm, Carl Sharpe, Kay and Ron Slusarenko, and Edward L. Ullman.

Work on the final stages of the book in 1972 was aided by a travel and study grant from The Ford Foundation; and by the cheerful assistance of Marilu Dauer and Ann Hassett in typing, checking, editing, and referencing the manuscript; and by Lyn Bruner for indexing the book.

I am also grateful to Senior Editor Brenda Gilchrist for constant support and attention to the book's production; to Harriet Bee for meticulous copy-editing; and to Cherene Holland and Helen Strodl for their help in shepherding many final details.

Grady Clay
Louisville, Kentucky
December 15, 1972

No TRUE SECRETS are lurking in the landscape, but only undisclosed evidence, waiting for us. No true chaos is in the urban scene, but only patterns and clues waiting to be organized.

All that we may soon become, our future, is out there shifting about, more or less ready to be found. Strange objects heave themselves into view and give off odd signals; familiar actors change costumes and shift roles; the action moves; the tempo changes. Cities, in short, are forever rewriting their repertoires.

And where are we? Grasping at straws, clutching yesterday's program, swamped by today's expert view, clawing at the newest opinion polls, but neglecting that limitless, timeless, boundless wealth of visible evidence that merely waits in a potentially organizable state for us to take the hard look, to make the next move. Experts may help assemble data, specialists may organize it, professionals may offer theories to explain it. But none of these can substitute for each person's own leap into the dark, jumping in to draw his or her own conclusions (fig. 1).

Full of booby traps is that darkness, but one must leap into one's own scene before uncovering the unity and continuity that lie half hidden in everyday happenings and workaday views. Whole industries of propagandists, many armed with official powers, push and shove to intrude their views ahead of our own. But none of these can match the power of the public's collective eye and its visual consensus.

Introduction

1. "What you see is what you get" arm patch.

In this book I offer assertions, short cuts, mental games, and other tools; I propose ways to grapple with everyday, visible, accessible evidence of the so-called urban revolutions of our time. My examples are chosen from everyday events and familiar objects, the happenings and places of ordinary life, from the street rather than from the laboratory. All these can and should be tested, criticized, improved upon or modified. I hope this effort will encourage others to look at urban change in more organized ways.

This is the book I needed but could never buy, a kind of Baedeker to the commonplace. It arose out of my experiences as an urban journalist and professional observer. In 1949, I had returned to daily reporting on *The Louisville Courier-Journal* after a year's Nieman Fellowship at Harvard University, filled with new questions about places and situations I sought to cover. How does one come to grips with a changing landscape where old divisions between city and country are fast disappearing? What are the quick navigational fixes? Why had no one written this book for *me?*

What a journalist seeks may often turn out to be needed by many others such as newcomers, migrants, travelers, tourists, families finding familiar places undergoing changes; and by students, street people, opportunists of every sort exploring new markets, niches, and realms. Each must get the hang of things, case new situations, dig the scene, get it all together, make sense. Are there universal methods we might use to speed up the process?

Gradually I learned how each person develops his or her own yard-sticks, insights, and mental tools for sorting things out, anticipating what comes next, and, finally, for conveying these discoveries to others.

In the process, I found that psychologist George A. Kelly had developed, and published in 1955, his own evidence and theory to show how the ordinary person, untrained in formal science, is his own best organizer against the propaganda, rumors, and clichés being mass-produced about his environment. Kelly argues, in *A Theory of Personality: The Psychology of Personal Constructs*, that each person builds a mental picture of the world, and then proceeds to continually modify, rebuild, and reconstruct it.[1] We do not merely react and respond to environment; we actively represent it and construe it—and thus build alternative constructions on it.

Kelly proposes that "every man is, in his own particular way, a scientist . . . ever seeking to predict and control the course of events in which he is involved."[2] He does this by trying the world on for size, forever seeking a better fit, not merely to enjoy the moment but also to predict and control his surrroundings better. He is concerned not so much with being well-tailored as with being a survivor.

And so I had begun putting together simple word tools, using what anybody can see to supplement such common journalistic sources as interviews, public hearings, statistics, events, gossip, scholarly studies, etc. I saw this as a device for shifting from "that's-what-the-man-said" reporting to "that's-what-I-saw" journalism.

Increasingly, I found it essential to look for patterns behind the single event, to ask not only the journalistic question "Why did *this* happen?" but the deeper question "Why do *such things as these* happen?" The usually reliable sources were not up to the task. Architectural history and criticism, for example, too often turned into a picture story of Great Buildings by Famous Architects. Critical analysis too often turned into a veiled bitchiness that dealt with personality conflicts among designers and critics. But the complex ways in which places worked, the uncovering of how they came to be, an analysis of their happenings, pace, and intensity—seldom did such inquiry fit into the neat chapters in standard texts. Nor were answers easy to come by in the filing-cabinet system of college courses and research specialization.

Neither were the gaps easily filled by the behavioral scientists, although this situation had begun to change by the late 1960's as radicalized graduates in architecture, planning, and the social sciences moved into the vacuum. New work in environmental cognition, cognitive mapping, perceptual analysis, and symbolic and pattern languages is beginning to make itself widely felt as it gets translated and tested. Many new user studies, aimed at finding out more exactly how people employ the environments they inhabit, have been put on display at conferences of the Environmental Design Research Association in the United States and at sessions of the Architectural Psychology Association in England.

Early in this search, I realized how little most Americans can find out about the evolution of their own, ordinary local surroundings. We bulldoze scenes and buildings of the past when they no longer pay their way in current cash. The typical, downtown big-city American building site, I would estimate, has been re-used at least four times since 1800, but dependable records of such shiftings are hard to come by. Most American cities are so grossly under-studied, most urban scenes so short-lived, that every person's own memory becomes a historic record, especially west of the Mississippi and in mushrooming suburbias.

I came to regard cities and their urbanizing regions as consisting of time as well as materials, and forever changing. This is the real continuity. There is no universal and everlasting right way for cities to present themselves to us. Each reflects the ideas, traditions, and energies available to its citizens in past centuries, as well as at this moment. Each landscape and townscape is an intricately organized expression of causes and effects, of challenges and responses, of continuity and, therefore, of coherence. It all hangs together, makes sense, fits one way or another— for good or bad, loosely or tightly. It has sequences, successions, climaxes. It reveals patterns and relationships forming and re-forming.

Some of these energetic scenes can be described in purely visual or stagecraft terms; or through the consensus of human emotional responses, in Gallup polls of what can be verbalized; or in structural or sequential terms. Some scenes we can experience only by moving through them. And some we may sense only in retrospect.

Thus, I have set about describing aspects of a unique phenomenon: the North American city as it may be seen in the 1970's. Deliberately, I have chosen almost all examples from the United States. Its cities share some 150 years of expanding energies, freedom for social experimentation and profitable exploitation of natural resources, staggering and careless growth, and competitive skulduggery mixed with farsighted organization.

With such increasing energies at our command—or out of control—we come headlong into conflict with nature. The story of the city is an account of how mankind has used new wealth and energy to exploit the natural world; the end of the story might describe the end of cities as we have known them.

Differences between places are being wiped out, and these are what we miss. New differences between places arise, and these we find disturbing. It is widely lamented that the difference between city and countryside is being eliminated by look-alike billboards, service stations, and other mass-produced commercial tackle and industrial apparatus.

Yet the remodeling and re-use of places is as predictable as the slow aging of a seemingly more stable familiar landmark. We watch a field being bulldozed, leveled, trenched, sewered, paved, and apartmented—a process as foreseeable on its own terms as is the gradual emergence of a historic civic district or a reconstructed Williamsburg, Virginia. Each scene follows rules of appearance and behavior observable over time; and in each there is change, decay, replacement, adjustment, and new uses for new times.

This suggests how to look at old differences between city and country. Real countryside, whatever that once meant, is supposed to contain real country activities, but surely no factories. Or so one might think—forgetting those thousands of New England and southern mill towns and western mining towns dotting the back country and remote valleys. Real country has always been a place of heavy work, and today's heavy work is increasingly done in prefabs located in suburbs, cornfields, and deserts in response to quite real commuting patterns, freight costs, and land access. There is a vast world-wide sorting-out process under way. Unfamiliar goings on crop up in unexpected places. There is hardly any real country left, especially east of the Mississippi if one defines "country" as territory

2. The majority of urban places represented by circles on this map were visited and photographed by the author. The remainder are represented on maps or are mentioned prominently in the text.

devoid of urban influences; and the so-called edge of the city has become a complex zone of contention extending in some instances for hundreds of miles. The rightful place of nature in this scene is endlessly debated and remarkably subject to disruption by expanding urban energies.

So it is foolish to yearn for a settled stability of scene that never existed. The shifty relationship between people and the landscape is not yet fully understood; their wheelings and dealings do not stand still for such methodological examination as befits the laboratory, nor am I the one to administer such scientific procedure. Consequently, I have tried to link direct observations in a personal way, which may incite others to more rigorous procedures.

In these observations, I have deliberately chosen words, notably in the chapter titles, that are short, memorable, sprinkled with hard consonants (I am a "K" man, myself), and conjure up vivid mental images. This reinforces my conviction that the language of cities need not be architectural or abstract, and it surely must not be deliberately complicated. Urban futures may be difficult, but they need not be rendered indescribable.

MOST AMERICANS are captives of an object-ridden language which they must awkwardly manipulate to deal with a changeable, processful thing called city. They speak of "downtown" as a place, but it is many places, scenes of overlapping actions, games, competitions, movements. There are many towns: downtown, uptown, crosstown, in town, out-of-town, old- and newtown, smoketown, honkytown, shantytown (fig. 3). A city is not as we perceive it to be by vision alone, but by insight, memory, movement, emotion, and language. A city is also what we call it and becomes as we describe it (fig. 4).

The approach I recommend for grappling with this changeling is a dedication to firsthand observation of phenomena, together with a loosening of our language. One must use artistic license freely, for "in the arts, the desire to find new things to say and new ways of saying them is the source of all life and interest."[1] Such a language will encourage a continuing watchful encounter with the changing environment. It lets us deal with this thingy process called urbanization, offers insight into energy-exchange systems and into processes as they wax and wane. Putting words to places, and handles to processes is a first step toward getting unlost and well-founded. We must watch for the before and after, the

Word-game

---

3. *"In cities as swiftly growing and composed of as diverse a population as Chicago, the problem of urban interpretation stands out in bold relief."* — Anselm Straus in Images of the American City (*Free Press of Glencoe, 1961*).

4. The way in which anyone looks at this scene is influenced by the class of language he chooses to describe it, and also by the social class attitudes from which that language derives. What goes on within the scene goes on, regardless.

CAPTION OPTION I

A Pollution

B Ugly scars on the landscape

C Jarring mechanistic shapes

D Dominating railroads & highways

E Billboard blight

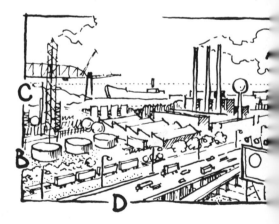

CAPTION OPTION II

A Production & power landmarks

B Symbols of the age

C Dynamic sculpture

D Supporting circulation arteries

E Advertising messages

goings on as well as the objects themselves. After detailed perception studies in American cities, David Lowenthal and Marquita Riel conclude that "only language provides the wealth of detail and nuance that enables us to identify and assess perceived differences among places."[2] Rudolf Arnheim has said, "You have to go back to the object—the way it seems, the way it feels, the way it is,"[3] and never stop there but keep going beyond the object to its surroundings and actions, asking "What goes on here?" and "What happens next?"

The true language of cities deals with relationships rather than free-standing objects. Maurice Merleau-Ponty, the French philosopher and cofounder of *Le Temps Moderne,* has observed that language "is understood only through the interaction of signs, each of which, taken separately, is equivocal or banal, and makes sense only by being combined with others."[4] Thus with the objects and processes in a city: each makes sense in combination, in relation to, in context, in time. Standing alone, each, considered on its own merits, is bereft, uncomplicated, and uncommunicative.

This was the root of much footless urban criticism of the early 1960's when solving city problems was said to require "total architecture," which seemed to mean replaying an old scene with new buildings. Architects themselves, stuck with old stage settings, had little to do with most of the urban environment, and surely not with *where* and *how* most city activities would go on. Annual guidebooks to the convention city of the American Institute of Architects treated each city as a collection of buildings by members of its guild. Seldom before the Houston guide of 1972 did such books recognize major forces that conditioned both buildings and human activity in that city.

I must confess to having sampled a huge cross section of these architectural/urbanist texts, and to having enjoyed the company of many of their authors while looking for insights which linked to my own experience. In the end, I have had to develop my own wordgame for coming to grips with city life—a playful, watchful approach, open-minded both to words and to their referents. One must relax, let the words hang loose and take up their own new and often awkward-appearing positions. And one must keep it up, fitting, comparing, and reshaping—mindful of the history of language but alert to meanings that are evolving and emerging. Neither language nor landscape stands still for us.

This game requires us first to master a discipline, and then. to learn its rules; but also to look for ways to stretch and bend the rules so as to maintain our own interest and inventiveness. In this context Michael J. Ellis's definition of play is a good one: "arousal-seeking behavior that leads to an increasing complexity of the players and their play."[5]

In a fast-changing situation, we must see, smell, feel, and deal; our language must respond, not resist. A young, television-broadcaster friend describes a new Louisville restaurant occupying a much sought-after site on the banks of the Ohio River: "And there is the Kingfish, sitting right on prime time (fig. 5)."[6] Another friend describes his research office, competing for a Midwest contract, as being "stacked up in a holding pattern over Kansas City."[7] Such analogizing, transference of image from one field to another, is vital in dealing with changing urban situations.

Putting together words in new ways is a means of putting together one's new world, a game at which ordinary people excel. Dwight Bolinger observes how creative the man in the street is at word building, especially when he uses verbs such as to help out, to write up, to die off, to string along, to gad about (fig. 6).[8] Ronald Slusarenko reports that wine-drinking hobos prefer to "jungle-up" on the wooded banks of the Willamette River in Portland, Oregon.[9] These phrasal verbs, as used in everyday speech, are "probably the most prolific source of new nouns in English," says Bolinger, since they so easily convert to "sit-in, wade-in, love-in, dropout, lockout, fallout, cookout, freakout, hangup, spin-off."[10]

5. "Sitting on prime time" is a phrase used by television commentator to describe Ohio River restaurant designed like side-wheel steamboat, which occupies a prime downtown site with high-rise hotel and bank tower (in background)—a phrase transferred from time-sales to geographic description.

6. Wordgame as played by sign painter: a phrase like "to hook up a trailer" gets shortened and verbalized as "hook-ups," at Amelia Island, Florida—outdoor evidence of language in the act of being changed. It describes the new, instant plug-in communities of trailers, travel trailers, and mobile homes.

Part of the game is in welcoming ill-fitting, odd-sounding, and allusionistic words, which, when applied out of context or in unaccustomed ways, send out sparks and flashes of insight. Wordgamesters learn to hang in there with new meanings, and not get hung up by discordant fits between old words used in new ways. Players train themselves away from literalness, monkey around with metaphors, live experimentally with the odd or unfamiliar, and even temporarily abandon texts and dictionaries in working through new meanings. New words can father new thoughts. As the literary critic George Steiner has observed, "Metaphor ignites a new arc of perceptive energy. It relates hitherto unrelated areas of experience."[11]

One must also describe in order not to despair. Paul Klee, the Swiss artist, somewhere has said, "I create . . . in order not to cry." Description, if free enough and accurate enough, suggests actions we should undertake to deal further with what we see.

Prescription—the putting together of proposals, why don't you's, solutions—depends on one's ability first to observe a problem, to describe it, and finally to propose solutions in language that is persuasive, if not eloquent, and firmly anchored to evidence from daily life.

This is no game to be played just for the hell of it, but for survival. Unless we all learn to say what we see, to describe it so others can see it, and to expand our own powers of description in a changing world, there is little reason to think we will do well at prescription, at finding solutions, at coping. Fuzzy language leads to fuzzy thoughts. The so-called "urban dialogue" of our time is not only dull but often hysterical. Its language is an awkward mixture of elitist architectural terms, of radical shitslinging, and of the manipulative lingo of evangelistic bureaucrats. You can read for pages or listen for hours, and have no contact with the hard facts of a living environment. Somehow we need to work out a better fit between language and environment. I think this can only happen if we continually confront the thing itself—the changing city, its people and their processes. Testing, testing, testing . . .

Fix 1: Perspective

MOST OF US still look outward from rigidly conditioned points of view. Our visual gyroscopes, set spinning centuries ago, cause us to swerve, pause before familiar scenes, and resist the new and unfamiliar. We are fixed or, in the earliest meaning of that word, fastened or pierced, stuck to an old constraint (fig. 7).

Of all the fixatives still permeating the modern vision, the perspectivist tradition is one of the most rigidifying. Like a mental chemical, it tends to preserve our perception in an earlier state—a kind of tunnel vision.

I recall being part of the voluble and amiable Delos III Symposium, a group of touring discussants brought together in 1965 by the Greek planner-architect Constantinos Doxiadis. On the Aegean island of Thassos we were wending our way up the mile-and-a-half climb to the Temple of Apollo for a memorable lecture by Dr. Arnold Toynbee. Along the way I had stopped to photograph the lovely crescent harbor below with its red-roofed village in the middle distance, greenish-blue mountains in the far distance, and setting sun casting its beams over the Aegean Sea just at the nose of the mountains, all enframed in pine branches (fig. 8).

For a moment I thought I was alone until I discovered the teen-aged son of our host sitting in an ancient crypt behind me. Young Apostolos Doxiadis was sketching the selfsame view that had stopped me in my tracks. Suddenly I realized that we both were captives of a 400-year-old

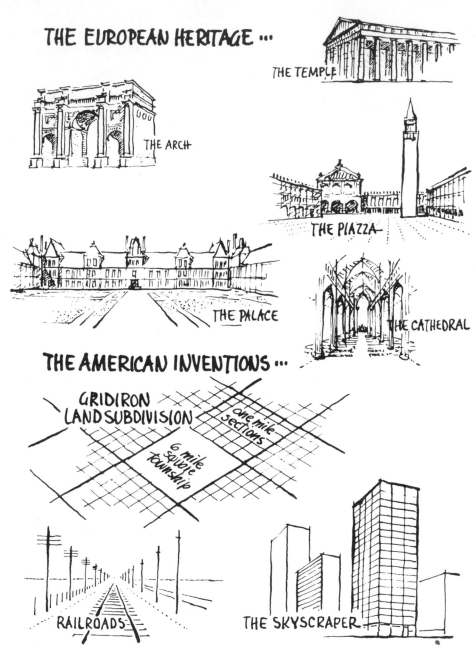

THE EUROPEAN HERITAGE ...

THE TEMPLE

THE ARCH

THE PIAZZA

THE PALACE

THE CATHEDRAL

THE AMERICAN INVENTIONS ...

GRIDIRON LAND SUBDIVISION

one mile sections

6 mile square township

RAILROADS

THE SKYSCRAPER

7. *Much depends on the viewer's personal "fix." Those whose world view is fixated in reverence for a golden age of palaces, piazzas, cathedrals, and temples will describe a scene of American inventions as monotonous, tacky, commercialized, etc.*

way of looking at the world, as a stage setting, tied to the perspectivist tradition, and magnetized to that particular spot and to no other. As Marshall McLuhan was later to put it, we were still prisoners of the Renaissance way of looking outward, "a piazza for everything and everything in its piazza,"[1]—visible, predictable, and static.

Later, home from Thassos, I was assembling an array of Kodachrome slides for a lecture on the principles of waterfront development only to discover, as I slouched over the light table, that each scene had been photographed from the same viewpoint as in Thassos: land was on the left, water on the right; the crescent of the water's edge ran from upper-right center downward. No matter where I had stationed myself, at home or abroad, my "fix" was showing (fig. 9).

What invisible hand had guided mine to produce those uniform photographs? It was indeed the perspectivists, those innovative artists of the fifteenth and sixteenth centuries who discovered and developed that powerful instrument of vision, the perspective drawing. For over 200 years, artists and mathematicians experimented to produce a sense of three-dimensional space in two-dimensional drawings. By the sixteenth century, the study of architectural perspective "became almost a theatrical extravagance, evidenced in the theater, in paintings and in architectural interiors."[2] (See figs. 10 and 11.)

8. We choose scenes to photograph according to the way we have been taught to see the world. This is the "correct" view westward across the Bay of Thassos in the northern Aegean—a view conditioned by centuries of the perspectivist tradition. It puts American tourists and the scenery in predictable relationship.

9. *Entrapment by custom and tradition: if you are accustomed to looking for landscape that falls into the "right" arrangement, this is what you are likely to get—a series of look-alike snapshots of the world.*

STVDIOSIS OPTICES
SPECTATORIBVS.

IPſe ego,qui primis Artem veneratus ab annis,
  Hoc ſtudui, vt nullum tempus abiret iners.
Grata oculis animóque fuit dîa Optica noſtris,
  Atque animo acceſſit qui facit eſſe, labor.
Hanc etenim per luſtra octo ſtudioſius artem
  Excolui. ſtudio, quod doceo, obtinui.
Dicitur ars certa hæc pariat quam regula certa:
  Traditur hîc certis Optica docta modis.
Ars regit hæc oculos, animos recreátque videndo:
  Non oculos falſis ludit imaginibus.
Exacté ſculptis ars hîc propoſta figuris,
  Vt veſtris oculis gratius eſſet opus.
Fórté aliquod nomen mihi erit:ſed Belgica docta,
  Si quod nomen erit, quærat & ipſa ſibi.
Hæc ſi grata oculis;occurret maior imago:
  Hanc exornatam pagina multa dabit.

10, 11. "This is my visage," wrote Jan Vredeman de Vries, sixteenth-century Dutch architect-painter-engraver. "My eyes and mind took pride in sacred Optics . . . forty years I plied this art devoutly." His last great work, Perspective: The Most Famous Art of Eyesight *(1604–5), demonstrated how to describe scenery according to rules of perspective. These engravings are from his book.*

Stereotyped ways of looking became the standard stance of the educated classes in Europe. "Gentlemen of the seventeenth century . . . having learned the clues to scenery from looking at pictures . . . were prepared to look for the picturesque wherever they found it . . . [depending on] the scenery's capability of being formed into pictures."[3]

Such fixes, organized out of the past, assume powerful influence, as in the work of Camillo Sitte, the Viennese architect whose *City Planning According to Artistic Principles* was immensely popular when published in 1899, and has become a standard reference.[4]

Like many a contemporary critic, Sitte made "an alarmed outcry of a cultured and sensitive citizen about the disturbing urban developments of his day."[5] He analyzed Greek, medieval, and Renaissance cities "to bring forth something of the old masterpieces," seeking out, "as technician and artist, the elements of composition which formerly produced such harmonious effects."[6] (See fig. 12.)

Since proper perspective has everything all lined up in three dimensions with no questions asked, no answers are needed; it is already taken care of in the picture, laid out neat and proper. We need do nothing about it. No demands on us, no intervention required of us, a limited relationship is set up between us. That is the end of a vital visual language—when it creates pictures that need no answers. And that also is the death

12. Looking back into the Middle Ages, when energy was in short supply, Camillo Sitte concluded that monumental buildings were best situated "on the sides of public squares of average spaciousness" so as to be looked at from a convenient distance, and because this saved builders the expense of adding fancy façades all around the structure (Sitte, The Art of Building Cities, p. 17).

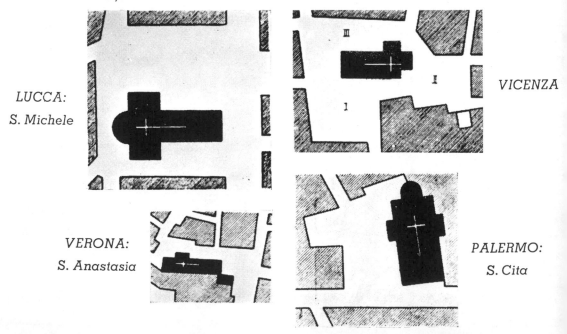

LUCCA:
S. Michele

VICENZA

VERONA:
S. Anastasia

PALERMO:
S. Cita

of a townscape—when it produces pat visual answers that require no questions.

Thus, by the 1950's when the United States was getting into its largest building boom, when housing, redevelopment, and suburban sprawl began to preoccupy American writers on urban affairs, many of us concentrated on the city in terms still visually organized by the perspectivist tradition. Gordon Logie, the British architect-planner, in his book *The Urban Scene,* dealt with towns and cities "from one particular point of view, their success or failure as pieces of scenery—one could almost say as sets in a theater."[7]

The most influential practitioners were English, notably Gordon Cullen whose brilliant prose-and-pen style, inventiveness in examining evidence firsthand, and ability to give readers a feel for the "thereness" of places had international impact. His perceptive book, *Townscape,* available in the United States in 1961, and his earlier writings and sketches in *The Architectural Review* set up a new vocabulary of serial vision (fig. 13).[8] His sketchbooks gave a clear sense of what it is like to move through neighborhoods. Although he dealt with the new sense of mobility, his ideal city seemed to be a medieval clustering of hobbledehoy buildings and winding alleys and streets. He projected so powerful a context in his sketches that it overshadowed much of his inventive, mobile gamesmanship for dealing with cities.

Traditional viewing of cities as stage settings and visual compositions dies hard. In her 1968 book, *The Language of Cities,* Fran P. Hosken dealt with the city mostly in such old-style terms of European theatrics as: order and unity, scale and space, light and shadow, color and texture.[9] Predictably, in such books today's cities fail to measure up. Even the contemporary landscape architect Lawrence Halprin, in his 1963 book, *Cities,* seemed to be stuck with the old townscape shopping list —nostalgic encounters with street furniture, urban pavement details, fountains.[10] However, at the very end of this book he broke loose with an adventurous choreography, "movement notations," later expanded in his 1970 book, *RSVP Cycles,* into the concept of scoring movements through the environment, a new intellectual confrontation with urban processes.[11]

Lurking among us still are feisty rear guards defending the older perspectivist tradition. They mutter that highway drive-ins are messy, signboards low class, suburbs lifeless, and that industrial districts are contemptible unless they copy the moated and turreted castles on the hill of the Middle Ages, surrounded by protective open fields, sentry posts, gates, and other medieval tackle (figs. 14 and 15).

Only when we manage to break loose from the old fixes and look with new vision will the city fully come alive to our presence in it. Only then can we fully recognize functions, goings on, competition, cooperation—

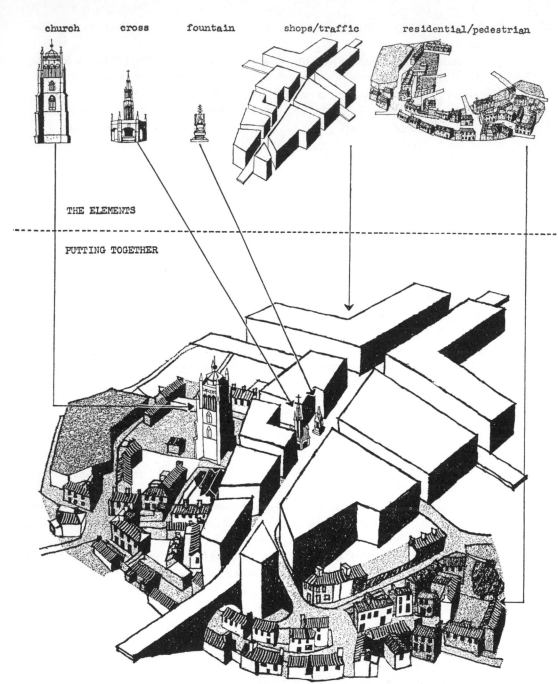

church cross fountain shops/traffic residential/pedestrian

THE ELEMENTS

PUTTING TOGETHER

13. *Breaking the old English town of Shepton Mallet into its components, Gordon Cullen argues that such exploration permits "a deeper penetration into the truth of the situation," especially by moving through it as a pedestrian (Townscape, p. 214).*

the energetic processes of city life too often concealed by the stage settings of the Renaissance and current efforts to copy them.

Furthermore, the burden of the Watts-to-Washington, D.C. riots of
the 1960's, fears of mob violence and of official repression, the looming
presence of domestic poverty and of increased governmental surveillance,
and the growing gap between American claims to moral purity and the
immorality of its violence abroad—all this served to traumatize too many
of us into a cynical nearsightedness when looking at the world. When it
was discovered that Lake Erie was dead—a discovery like Mark Twain's
death, somewhat premature—too many otherwise perceptive Americans
shut their minds to a continuing analysis of that complex water system
and its behavior setting. It was more satisfying to condemn than to investigate, simpler to look, only to look away.

But I do not think steady trauma is a healthy state, nor the dour puri-

*14. Opened in 1969, the Cummins Technical Center at Columbus, Indiana,
world headquarters of the Cummins diesel engine empire, echoes medieval
castle settings—Haw Creek, in foreground, straightened and cleared of brush
by company, building upon filled land to stay above floods, all access concentrated at the side and rear.*

15. *Traditionalists may insist that contemporary American industrial layouts copy the moated and turreted castles of the Middle Ages surrounded by fences, protective open fields, friendly neighbors, etc. Anheuser-Busch brewery north of Columbus, Ohio.*

tanical glower a receptive stance. All gatherings are not potential mobs, all gleaming waters are not to be scrutinized exclusively for oil slicks, nor all forests penetrated merely for proof of corporate clear-cutting. There are pleasures as well as crimes to be uncovered, distinctions to be made, and prospects to be explored, described in clear detail, and understood.

Fix 2: Cross Sections

If only cities, like insects, could hold still like good specimens while we pin them to the laboratory table for study! If only they were like cadavers: cold and rigid from the freezer so that anatomists could debate, following the lead of Andreas Vesalius in the sixteenth century,[12] the proper way to cut a cross section and examine the anatomical patterns inside.

The cross-section examination is an ancient device for studying almost anything from insects to regions, and that great biologist, Sir Patrick Geddes, has left us a superb example in his valley section. It worked well as a pictorial image in his day, and was most clearly put forward in his famed Cities Exhibition at Chelsea, London, in 1911.[13] Geddes had exhibited a large painting of a typical valley cross section as a visual device for understanding the unity and complexity of that geographic unit.

Travel with old Sir Patrick in mind, starting as he did at a remote mountainside, descending through woods, pastures, fields, outer suburbs and then into the town and its seaside docks. It was a predictable set of places, which Geddes perceived in simplistic panoramic terms; the town was a product of its region. From its neighboring hills flowed coal to be shipped, game to be eaten, cattle to be slaughtered, wheat to be milled—everything proceeding downward from hills and fields to grocer, miller, baker, brewer, and shipper. The town was the local magnet, the processor of raw materials that were raised, found, dug, or grown nearby.

Thus Geddes perceived the early twentieth-century town region as a unit. His cross-section diagram enabled him and his exhibition audience to see towns and cities as the expression of their settings. His 1911 panorama showed an orderly, progressive system of transactions from uplands to port, from raw to finished materials. The town or city was still the receiver of raw materials, messages, goods, instructions, and influence from its hinterland.

But how does one translate that old intellectual device today? The contemporary urban complex has become the major power source, the originator of organization, the sender of messages, the manufacturer of influence. Its major exports are energy and control. It ships out regulations, orders, information, propaganda, and directives. It generates transactions to be carried out by the city's agents, salesmen, bureaucrats, managers, and owners. The city is a source region, as polar Canada and Siberia are source regions for North America's weather fronts, spawning and giving identity to cold air masses that flow southeast across the United States.

This 180-degree shift in influence, from Geddes's day to this, has been traumatic. In three generations, "countryside" has been converted from source to recipient, from generator to subject, chattel, or pawn. Countryside is judged chiefly by the presence of, or lack of, urban goods, techniques, and influence. College curricula writers are hard pressed to insist there is still a legitimate subject called "rural sociology," and tend to speak instead of the rural-urban continuum. The prevailing view in America is outward from a city base of operations. Country takes its identity from the city rather than from its own self, and country life is increasingly hung up with nostalgic and usually denigrating images of itself created in Washington, New York, Boston, San Francisco, and other major image-generation centers.

Thus to view the city with anything resembling Geddes's perspective of the valley section is to misjudge its force, to misperceive its direction, and, above all, to be stuck with a mental tool that hardly equips us to grasp the dominance of city influence over the whole of American life and landscape. Geddes's analysis, like that of the perspectivists, is out of date; and those who hold to it steadfastly are ill-equipped to deal with, or to understand, the forces at work within the contemporary metropolitan scene.

Fix 3: Centrality

There was a time when everything that was important in a region happened at its center; when all roads led to the center (before the automobile made possible the discovery that all roads also led *away* from the center); and when the importance of one's home, business, office, showroom, and activities was measured by its proximity to that most central of all points, the old city center, the old downtown (fig. 16).

So powerful was this fixation that it has dominated city growth and attitudes toward cities for thousands of years. During most of those years, mankind had no choice: being physically "close-in" was the only way one could efficiently buy, sell, trade, barter, exchange, charm, seduce, or negotiate. Everything in urban life sooner or later had to flow, either physically or symbolically, through the central market places for goods, services, and ideas. Geddes's valley section reflected this flow.

Today, thanks to cheap or free media, to the new interconnected and intercommunicating, switched-on society, and to increased personal mobility and movement, the old grip of centrality is loosening. No longer can we be certain that, by the grace of God and the laws of geometry, all things of importance are best transacted at the center, all debates concluded at the center, and all great structures located at the center. The first nails in that coffin were supplied by the invention of the telegraph and telephone (which, among other things, put the skids under coffeehouses in New York as *the* places for swapping business information in the 1870's); by mass transportation to space for sale via street railways in cities, railroads, and automobiles; and now by the new personal media —portable TV, console access to computers, hotlines to libraries and data centers, and quick access to plugged-in information.

Just as the old concept of chastity has been structurally undermined by the Pill, so the old concept of centrality has been undercut by everyman's

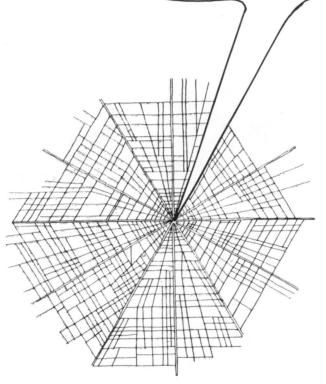

16. *The power of central focus; the old magic of centrality has disintegrated.*

access to space by movement (commuting, vacationing, long-range visit-ing, etc.), and by everyone's access to information that does not require face-to-face encounters for its production and possession.

For hundreds of years, royalty and other powerful groups had sought to tighten the reins on central places, to force the public to traffic through and with the center, to build at high densities and not sprawl at a dis-tance. But these containment efforts have generally failed, except in such

17

18

land-starved and crowded countries as Holland, where sprawl is rigidly prevented in order to save scarce farmland.

Consequently, it is time to recognize that the magic of centrality has waned; and that our fixation with the old concept of a city where "everything goes up in the center"—land values as well as skyscrapers —no longer provides an accurate view of the way cities are acting and changing. And so what happens to old downtowns now epitomizes something far bigger: traumatic changes and shifts in voting and financial power; the takeover of central neighborhood turf by blacks and other minorities; the restructuring of whole cities as they segregate shopping onto suburban strips and clusters, health care into medical centers, jobs into industrial and port districts, and many another single-purpose enclave in a more dispersed pattern (figs. 17 and 18).

To be sure, the rising power of government in many parts of the world, including the United States, continues to express itself in "efficient" and "rational" efforts to promote high-density centers, especially in master plans that try to restrict the growth of suburbs, and concentrate housing developments downtown.

But, just as the marvelous discovery of perspective gradually became perverted into stage setting, just as the cross section and its scientific uses led us to look at the city as a specimen to be frozen for laboratory examination, so the old magic of centrality has misled us into seeing the city only in terms of its ancient and once-immobile geometry. Each of these old-time fixes now tells us to get out and take a new look around.

17. *Large-scale economic segregation: strung out on huge open tract with new railroad and highway access is General Electric Company's Appliance Park East, the southern economic base of newtown Columbia, Maryland.*

18. *Hospitals in hayfields: the new decentralization of health care, doctors' offices, drugstores. In distance, suburban hospital and doctors' offices; in foreground, new 1972 hospital under construction. St. Matthews, Kentucky, vicinity Browns Lane, Breckinridge Lane, Interstate 64.*

SPECIAL PLACES in cities carry huge layers of symbols that have the capacity to pack up emotions, energy, or history into a small space. I call them epitome districts. Here one can see the bigger place in compression or in miniature; here one can say, "If you've seen one, you've seen them all." But no two are ever exactly alike.

In linguistics, an epitome is a brief statement expressing the essence of something, a short presentation of a large topic. A city's epitome districts are crammed with clues that trigger our awareness to the larger scene —things around the corner, processes out of sight, history all but covered up. They stand for other things; they generate metaphors; they are the sort of places that, ideally, help us get it all together.

The thing about epitome districts is that they seldom stand still. The symbolic load is forever shifting. One generation's epitome district may become the next generation's candidate for oblivion. Only a trace may survive—a persistent street pattern, a local accent, a cluster of intermeshed businesses. But do not picture epitome districts as remnants or mere reminders. They offer, I think, the most compelling evidence of present and future change, providing we know where to look, and how.

Epitome Districts

The term "epitome district" was first coined by a team of bright graduate students at the Medill School of Journalism of Northwestern University in 1966.[1] We were looking together for ways to grasp those changes
that were convulsing Chicago. The students tracked through the stockyards, then disintegrating like so many other old stockyards—in Denver,
Kansas City, Phoenix, and elsewhere—because of the pressure of rising
big-city expenses and the increased value of stockyard land for other,
better-paying activities. They looked at port-of-entry neighborhoods
crammed with newcomers, at a North Shore suburb with streets almost
wholly deserted at 10 A.M.; they uncovered an indicator of doubling-up
by tenants in old apartments (by counting makeshift mailboxes in the
beat-up lobby), a way to measure neighborhood density (by getting
out early in the morning after the first snow and counting footprints),
a way to check on family overcrowding (by looking for beat-up back
stoops and bare yards trampled by too many kids); and they observed
the awkward fit between old-timers in village houses amid giant new
suburban warehouses in Elk Grove Village and Wheeling, Illinois. And
in doing all this they came to see how the traditional fix on downtowns,
traditional information sources, and traditional city images are no longer
dependable. At first they found it hard to look. All their training had
taught them to track down key persons to interview—mayors, city engineers, county political chairmen, et al. They were accustomed to trust a
quote, but not a sight. Only after many weeks were they able to use what
they *saw* as skillfully as what they had been told.

Let us look, then, for our own epitome districts; places where one may
observe formal and informal rituals, symbolic activities: the organization
of folk festivals ranging from parades to inaugurations, from unveilings
to auctions to rallies to funerals and swearings-in. Places where such
activities begin are key places to all the other activities that feed into
and out of those places—especially caravans, parades, motorcades, and a
host of proliferating processions that jam up traffic in every city. The
beginning point—historically and at the moment—is a special sort of epitome district.

In many cities, one can pick out such ceremonial places easily. In the
South there is a modest old Confederate monument as one's guide; in
the North a monument is similarly located but two or three times as big
(losers generally cannot afford big monuments to lost wars). In older
gridiron-type cities, it is likely to be at the City Hall grand staircase. In
suburban towns, celebrations begin at a major shopping center. (The
1972 political campaigns offered scores of examples of candidates hus-
tling for suburban votes by helicoptering in and out of shopping-center
parking lots.)

Once we become sensitized to origins, to beginning-places, to places of

SYSTEMATIC LAND SUBDIVISION
SQUARE **GRIDIRON** PATTERN

CHICAGO

UNSYSTEMATIC
LAND SUBDIVISION
IRREGULAR
PATTERN

19

20

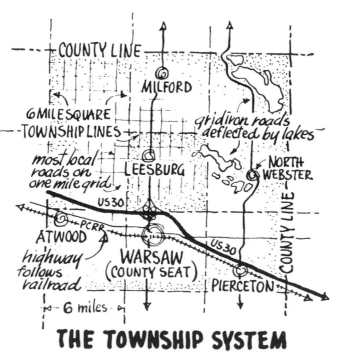

COUNTY LINE

MILFORD

6 MILE SQUARE
TOWNSHIP LINES

*gridiron roads
deflected by lakes*

*most local
roads on
one mile grid*

LEESBURG

NORTH
WEBSTER

US 30

PCRR

ATWOOD

WARSAW
(COUNTY SEAT)

US 30

COUNTY LINE

*highway
follows
railroad*

PIERCETON

6 miles

THE TOWNSHIP SYSTEM
and one mile squares in northern Indiana

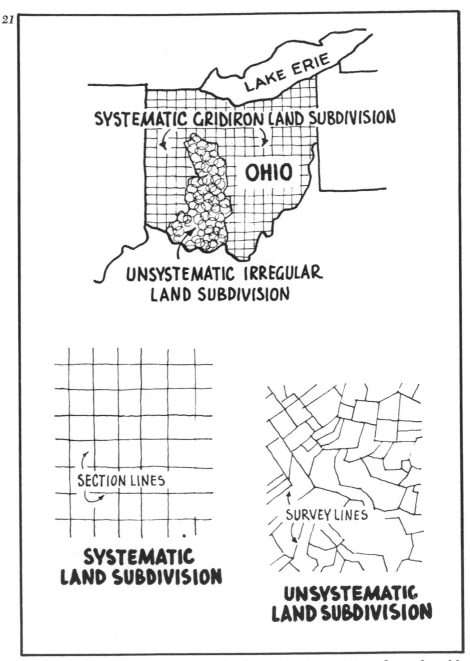

19, 20, 21. Giant-sized breaks in landscape patterns occur where the old national grid took over, generally west of Ohio and Mississippi rivers, with many historical and geographic variations beyond those shown on the United States map here. One of the clearest sets of breaks within one state is the old Virginia Military District within Ohio, subdivided after the Revolution. By far the larger part of the nation, however, falls into a predictable township system.

transition, we are then in a heightened state of awareness, not only to the processes of a city, but to those places especially rich in these directional and functional clues.

Breaks

A city's energies falter or shift gears in predictable ways and places. During a century and a half of rapid expansion, American cities have shown the results of change more clearly than have those of Europe, and these breakpoints—or gear-shifting zones—tell us a great deal about the larger scene. As special, geometric epitome districts, they offer quick insights into the larger dimensions of the city.

A "break," as I am using the term, occurs where there is an abrupt, visible switch in the direction and/or the design of streets—especially where the pattern shifts diagonally. It occurs usually where one gridiron of streets laid across flat land encounters a steep hill or a valley; or else where the original gridiron of one settlement, or one early surveyor, clashes with an adjoining street network. From this clash, there usually emerges a series of awkward, irregular, and angular street junctions along the fracture zone where the grids encounter each other (figs. 19, 20, and 21). No matter how long ago the clash took place (thousands of them occurred in the nineteenth century), the results are usually visible and influential today. Thus, to watch for breaks is to find clues to history as well as to current events.

Urban critics, particularly those hung up in the perspectivist tradition, insist that the American city is unvarying and monotonous in its addiction to the grid. But it is not enough to echo this stale lament; for to understand an American city on first contact, one must look beyond the individual grid to its interface or fracture zone with the next, and to variations within the grid (fig. 22). One need not swallow the line that all grids are alike, nor accept whole hog the assertion that one break is as good as another. Some breaks exert a positive effect on the development around them; others bitch things up on all sides. Few breaks exist with *no* apparent side effects; at least I have never found one in looking at dozens of cities and their street systems.

For example, I have gone back several times since 1963 to observe the modest dog-leg break between the older grid of Austin, Texas, and the slightly shifted and skewed grid to the north, where the University of Texas neighborhood begins at West Nineteenth Street (fig. 23). The north-south streets miss joining at Nineteenth Street by half a block. Consequently, anyone approaching Nineteenth Street looks directly at the backsides and hindquarters of the properties opposite. This particu-

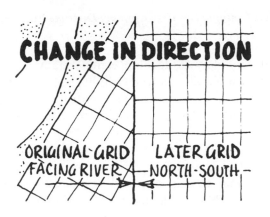

CHANGE IN DIRECTION

ORIGINAL GRID FACING RIVER

LATER GRID — NORTH-SOUTH —

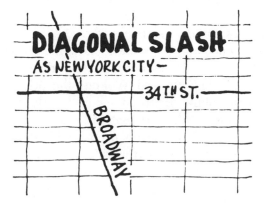

DIAGONAL SLASH

AS NEW YORK CITY —

34TH ST.

BROADWAY

23. *Between town and gown at Austin, Texas, Nineteenth Street forms a distinct geographic separation where two street patterns meet at the break, forming a series of irregular dog-leg intersections. These have influenced land uses and set up a zone of transition signals for motorists.*

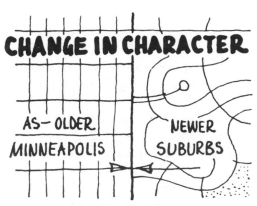

CHANGE IN CHARACTER

AS— OLDER MINNEAPOLIS

NEWER SUBURBS

BREAKS

22

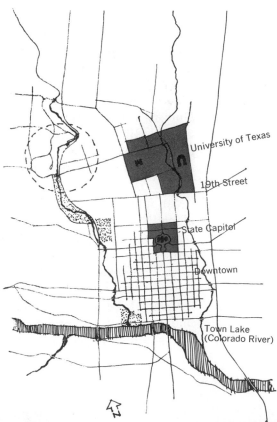

University of Texas

19th Street

State Capitol

Downtown

Town Lake (Colorado River)

larly uninviting break has been very slow to develop commercially, compared with most diagonal breaks which offer better visibility. The reason is not altogether aesthetic. Motorists are so preoccupied with negotiating the dog-leg junctions they pay little attention to the roadsides and what they might offer.

Sharp breaks tend to occur at the edge of central business districts, as though the energies which produced the first city have now exhausted themselves. Time and again, as one travels outward from old downtowns—as in Denver, San Francisco, New Orleans, Seattle, Fresno, Las Vegas, or Minneapolis—one confronts confusion: the grid turns angular and odd-cornered; it slopes off in a new direction (fig. 24). And along this zone of fractured intersections one encounters a new framework with different densities, architectural styles, building setbacks (fig. 25).

The most confusing break I have encountered is the remarkable razzle-dazzle no-man's-land area in downtown Denver where two disparate grids come together at Broadway, Twentieth, and Welton: the original diagonal grid that was based on the South Platte River and early railroads parallel to the river, and a subsequent grid that follows the compass directions: north-south, east-west. This lash-up occurs with devastating impact where the blocks are cut up into triangles. So confusing is this melange at first that there is no visible identity left. Most buildings in the vicinity have been razed, the multiple junction is surrounded by parking lots, few pedestrians are to be seen, and one-way traffic speeds through this man-made mini-desert.

Yet this apparent confusion reveals several patterns to a patient observer standing at the break. First, the older flatland grid to the west contains the bulk of old Denver's businesses. Secondly, east of this break you begin walking uphill—an exercise most downtowners have avoided, thus making the break a prime location for parking lots. Thirdly, the University Club and other remnants of the old mansion district along Capitol Hill to the east were obstacles to big-business development until the late 1960's. Now the slope is hot property, being filled with giant office buildings, a transition observable at the breaks of many other cities.

Austin and Denver illustrate the most familiar location for breaks—along the edges of the first settlement or original city plan. Most original plans consisted of rectangular lots formed into blocks, and these, in turn, formed into a rectangular gridiron. Almost inevitably, the first grid followed the alignment of an early bridge or was staked out at right angles to the first town landing or to the water's edge (fig. 26).

Original grids were seldom big enough for growth. Usually by the mid-nineteenth century, another set of speculating settlers laid out a new townsite just upriver or downriver from the original settlement. Seldom

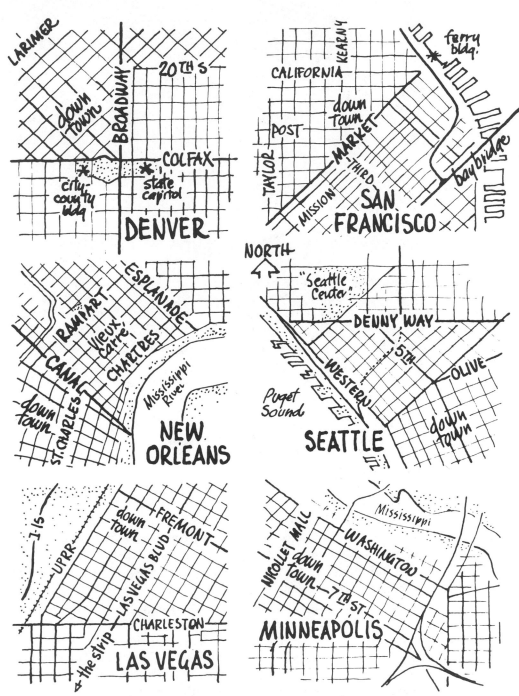

24. *Predictably, breaks in the gridiron pattern tell you where the original settlement ended and another, with a competing pattern, grew up next door. Most often the original gridiron was at right angles to a water landing. New Orleans' many grids follow the beds in the Mississippi River. Such breaks are handy navigation zones for getting one's bearings in a strange city.*

25. Confusing to strangers is the competition set up between two old settlement patterns, as here along state road 29 (Massachusetts Avenue) northeast of Indianapolis, Indiana. Parking lot lines in foreground follow the north-south dictates of the national grid, while Route 29 was laid out diagonally athwart the grid. Thus property lines, lot lines, and painted lines do a continual flipflop, shifting from grid to diagonal.

did the latecoming grid merge easily with the original. In New Orleans, each new wave of settlers appeared to spawn its own grid, anchored to a different loop or meander of the Mississippi River.

In Milwaukee in the 1840's, Juneautown settlers on the east side of the Milwaukee River settled on one gridiron, while the Kilbourntown folk on the west side had their streets following a different alignment. It took decades of legal skirmishes, bridge-burnings, and fistfights before the geopolitical break was mended.[2] Today, four downtown streets—Kilbourn, Wells, St. Paul, and East Buffalo—cross the narrow Milwaukee River on oddly-diagonal bridges as reminders of that historic break.

In the Midwest and Great Plains, the original grid offers an instant fix on the town's origins—usually anchored to the main railroad through town. Go to the point where the main street crosses the main track and that is where it all began. The grid determined early growth, and if the tracks ran northeast-southwest, so did the town. Eventually, as such towns expanded, their diagonal grids encountered the one-mile-apart range or section roads, which followed the north-south–east-west compass. At that point, the old railroad grid was abandoned, and beyond the one-mile roads, new streets shifted to follow the national grid, as at Norman, Oklahoma; Hays, Kansas (fig. 27); and Fresno, California.

Not quite so easy to observe is the original grid in Atlanta, which began as a railroad-grid town called Terminus. Today, that original grid and its small, almost-square blocks make up the heart of Atlanta's financial district, north of the old railroad gulch, and surrounded by breaks (fig. 28). "Underground Atlanta's" streets, with their huge granite-block sidewalks, follow the original pattern next to the railroad.

In Macon, Georgia, the breaks around the old downtown area go back to the Civil War. The town was left bankrupt, and its citizens were concerned more with survival than with perpetuating the original rectangular street plan of 1823. Postwar poverty led to the abandonment of the 180-foot right-of-way of the original numbered streets, and today one can

26. Typical evolution of a Midwest or western city with original landing place and first street gridiron at top. Later, land developers set up their own grid until finally, in Phase III, new streets joined the national grid and followed its N-S-E-W directions.

BREAK EVOLUTION

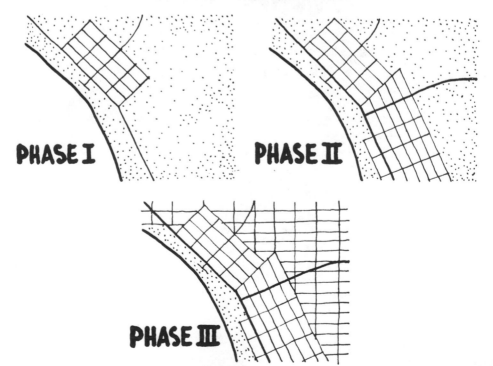

PHASE I

PHASE II

PHASE III

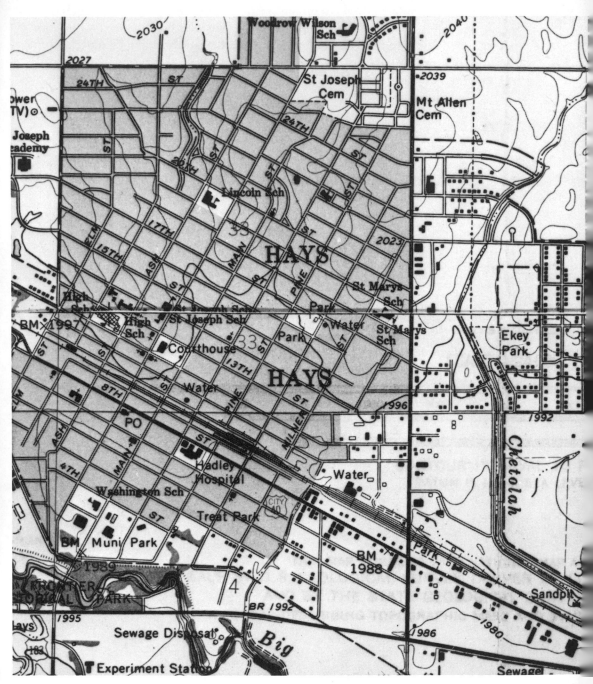

27. *Early railroad towns show their beginnings along the tracks with their rectangular patterns tightly anchored to, and determined by, the direction of the tracks. Here at Hays, Kansas, the tracks ran diagonally. As soon as the city's expansion reached the old mile-square section or range line roads, the gridiron "straightened up" into the national gridiron based on points of the compass.*

trace that war's influence by the sudden narrowing, bending, or twisting of many streets at the edges of the original grid.[3]

City dwellers have responded to breaks in remarkably uniform ways: as investors, settlers, and travelers they have resisted crossing the break either in home-seeking or investing. Breaks form psychological, as well as geographic, barriers; they set up relationships that confuse, so that territory on the other side seems strange and unreliable. Land beyond the break has an uneasy look about it; development is spotty and irregular.

28. *Atlanta's original gridiron of rectangular blocks was based on the early railroad, here running northwest-southeast across downtown. As city boomed, it set its streets on a new alignment, generally north-south. The old grid marks the heart of financial district.*

With a speculator's nose for locations, one can learn to look at civic centers, fairgrounds, and other large-scale enterprises for clues to the locations of old breaks. For example, the site of Seattle's "Century 21" World's Fair of 1962 was located just beyond, and north of, a major break in that city's two downtown grids. Land beyond the break, north of Denny Regrade, was still comparatively underdeveloped in the 1950's when the city sought, with a municipal bond issue, the 72-acre site that has now become a major cluster of civic buildings called Seattle Center. Thus, a location that was once beyond the pale, moved into center stage.

Mobility at the Breaks

High prices have always been paid for highly accessibile sites, and the junction of two diagonal streets has been exploited for its accessibility for thousands of years. Edmund N. Bacon's exposition of the Sixtus V plan for Rome in *Design of Cities* shows a sophisticated effort to create a movement system for that complex city, with a number of easy-access sites created at the nodes of traffic.[4] Bacon's account, in the perspectivist tradition, emphasizes the high visibility of these junctions; but the way traffic moves in Rome is proof, even today, that the key element was access rather than visibility alone. In a sense, Sixtus was an early break-maker, using the power of the Church to do what later and more mundane planners have done, often by default, with the simple geometry of disjointed grids. Break sites—if they are not altogether awkward, as in Austin, Texas—are valued for their unique accessibility in hundreds of cities.

Undiscovered and unexploited breaks, however, are easy targets for contemporary highway and urban-renewal scouts and for tidy-minded city planners anxious to regularize traffic flow. Thus many nineteenth-century breaks are getting buried beneath new expressways, superblocks, civic centers, and other large-scale ventures. Most breaks remain intact, however, and a casual inspection of any city will uncover a consistent pattern of break locations for prominent buildings such as nineteenth-century railroad stations.

Since railroad tracks often followed rivers, valleys, and other topographical breaks, the depot or union station generally occupies a strategic break site, often at the end of a major city street, as in Macon, Georgia; Portland, Oregon (fig. 29); and Kansas City, Missouri. Before they all disappear in the reorganization of passenger service brought on by Amtrak in the 1970's, they should be treasured as clues to the onetime "most accessible place in town." Their presence or disappearance is a clue to what is happening beyond their walls and tracks.

29. Scores of nineteenth-century union stations are quick and easy reference points, being at the edges of the old cities or along geographical breaks such as rivers. Portland's Union Station, its main axis paralleling the Willamette River, offers a quick fix at the north end of Sixth Street.

30. Spotting a break in street patterns at Kansas City, between old Missouri River–oriented grid and later gridiron to the south, highway planners chose this confusion zone as a location for Interstate 70–U.S. 24/40 east-west. Thus, highways and urban renewal have wiped out many breaks.

31. While expressways and urban renewal wipe out breaks in one part of the city, architects and institutions go to extreme lengths to overcome the monotony of the breakless gridiron pattern, as here at Columbus, Ohio, where the Grant Hospital School of Nursing on East Town Street has been set askew, on the diagonal. It thereby acquires some of the high visibility that normally accrues to buildings located on breaks.

Since breaks offer such incomparable building sites and planning opportunities, one would expect them all to become preserve-and-dramatize zones on city plans. Yet far too many planners and downtown business groups simply try to wipe out the break, shove it under an expressway (fig. 30), or destroy it with a renewal project. Thus, many a city's future can be previewed in what is happening today, in either the destruction or enhancement of these old breaks (fig. 31).

The Political Venturi

Quite by accident, mixed into a long search, I stumbled upon one of the more important epitome districts to be found in any city that is still linked together by an establishment, power elite, or power structure. This is the distinct pathway or network of paths along streets, sidewalks, and corridors followed by central-city movers and shakers, influentials, wheelers and dealers, and hangers-on.

Despite the rise of electronic communications, much important person-to-person business is still transacted out in the open, between office and lunch, courtroom and conference, bench and bar, desk and drinks.

The process of my own discovery is worth looking into, for it tells something about the ways in which downtown epitome districts work, and suggests clues to their futures. In writing about my own city, Louisville, I found it essential to move about on foot, to pay personal calls on as many political, financial, and other key figures as possible, to see them in their own haunts and lairs, to probe their attitudes and experience, and, as a journalist, to move in public places, observing who was with whom for clues to future alliances, deals, and consortia.

After repeated exposure, I discovered that one particular stretch of sidewalks, doors, and corridors in the financial-civic district was extraordinarily productive in contacts, tips, suggestions, reactions, observations, and gossip.

My discovery, it happened, took place on a Monday. My Mondays were highly pressured and competitive; days on which it was vital to catch up on potential news after a weekend. I found that by stationing myself at noon on the crowded public sidewalk outside the largest bank and office building, keeping in view the doors of the County Court House and the second-largest bank, plus the route from nearby City Hall, I was likely to meet at least two dozen news sources, men in public life or business, headed for lunch at restaurant or club, willing and sometimes eager to exchange rumor, gossip, and hard information. (One never approaches these encounters empty-handed or vacant-minded.) It became clear that here was an unavoidable "Indian path" between the offices of the downtown elite and their noonday drinking/lunching/negotiating places. This walkway carried a high information load, a mixture of rumor, gossip, facts, and near-truths having varying capacity to shock, inform, placate, and cause repercussions. It was, for my purposes, a highly volatile and explosive mixture to be handled carefully, professionally, and with due regard for the libel laws.

By analogy, I then compared it with the Venturi tube[5] of an automobile carburetor, that narrow aperture or nozzle through which a stream of gasoline was forced under pressure. Once through the nozzle, it expands quickly, mixing with air and vaporizing into an explosive mix to be compressed by the cylinder head, ready for the spark plug to force it to life. Thus the "venturi" is a gatherer, an accumulator, and accelerator of traffic, movement, and information.

The typical venturi of this sort seldom stretches longer than a fifteen-minute walk, although it is clear that executives will walk several times as far to lunch—especially in pairs or threesomes—as they will walk from their cars to their offices. The "throat" of the venturi may be only a few yards long and a sidewalk wide; it may split, disappear, and suddenly reappear. It has its popular corners, its Peacock Alleys, and its cargo of information which varies with the seasons and with demolition or new construction along its route. The formation of new men's clubs, the merger of new and old, and pressure to open all-white, male clubs to women and minorities indicate a situation that is far from static. Many a club withers on the downtown vine, while new ones sprout in the prospectuses of proposed new downtown skyscrapers. Atlanta's penthouse Commerce Club is so successful it has opened a branch some blocks away.

Although financial and court districts are the most immovable and traditional parts of the nineteenth-century American downtown, few of them are static. Competition is keen and transforming. Thus venturis and their appurtenances—the clubs, courts, banks, offices, bars, and restaurants—are epitomes of the larger city; they offer indicators of its power structure, strengths, and challenges. They are carriers of information, conveyors to be used, planned, controlled, and manipulated.

There is nothing more calculated to inspire the cupidity of speculators (and of more prudent investors) than a chance to create, and then monopolize, a local venturi—whether it is a single street that seems to be "the only way through town," or a town or city occupying a large-scale venturi location or geographic bottleneck of the sort described here.

This opportunity fascinated the banker on whose doorstep I had first discovered the process—so much so that in the new Citizens' Fidelity Bank tower in Louisville the ground-floor arcade has been consciously designed as a small-scale venturi to attract low-level customers, and the Jefferson Club added on the top floor to magnetize high-level decision-makers. Bank president Maurice D. S. Johnson plans, during the 1970's, to extend his bank's venturi diagonally southeastward into the heart of the city's shopping district—barely in the nick of time, for his competitor, the First National Bank, has attempted to create its own venturi two blocks north, with a forty-story office tower and a handsome plaza facing south toward the traditional venturi. No doubt the bankers' grapevine has been at work, for one may observe similar maneuvers elsewhere: the design of the new First National Bank in Chicago's Loop was carefully manipulated to pull customers through its giant arcade and off its own plaza on the sunny south side, and influentials to its Mid-Day Club on the fifty-sixth floor.

No venturi is immutable; some disappear as the information capacity of a downtown district shrivels. The "yield" of a political venturi changes with the seasons in varying degrees depending on latitude: few people hang around Chicago's sidewalks in midwinter, and I will be surprised if the grandiose South Mall at Albany, New York—built at a cost now approaching $1 billion—will be anything but a vast windswept wilderness. It is a truism among journalists that the level of interchange and gossip drops drastically around state capitols when the state legislatures adjourn; and similar changes occur when any population shift drains a local pathway system (figs. 32, 33, 34, and 35).

In order to grasp the dynamic forces at work, let us look into several venturi districts, beginning with Jacksonville, Florida: In ten years the old lunchtime venturi has been fragmented by the openings of the River Club (1955) and the University Club (1965), each one atop a new office tower a mile from old downtown on the opposite bank of the St. Johns River. By 1972, all but one major central hotel had closed, few top-flight restaurants remained, and an early venturi northward from the financial district to the old Seminole Club had thinned out. Whether a new insurance headquarters and proposed "skywalk" system might reverse the trend remains to be seen.

Columbus, Ohio: The junction of Third and East Broad streets provides the action scene, much of it still revolving around the State Capitol in mid-city. The University Club is just behind the Capitol on South Third, the Athletic Club at 130 East Broad, and the august Columbus Club a short walk east on Broad, where, in the early 1970's, it faced a major building boom across Broad where the new State Office Building, and Borden Company headquarters were high-rising. Close by an alley called Lynn Street blossomed out with the Pewter Mug and other dimly lit restaurants to reinforce the old Ringside restaurant.

In Hartford, Connecticut, the traditional venturi is anchored to the marble entry of the Hartford Club, an imposing red brick building with its rear quarters extensively rebuilt and a handy parking lot on the south side. Across Prospect Street is the huge Travelers' Tower Plaza (1960) and the Wadsworth Atheneum, the nation's first free art museum. The more modest University Club, tucked away on narrow old Lewis Street a few minutes' walk to the west, is less big-business oriented. Members of the State Legislature and other politicians are magnetized, by good food and a staff that memorizes their names, to Carbone's, a bleak-looking but popular drive-in restaurant on Franklin Avenue a mile south of the business district and considered too far away to walk (fig. 36).

Cincinnati, Ohio: The south side of Fourth, between Walnut and Main, is considered "on the way" from important downtown offices to both the Queen City Club and the University Club. Major banks provide generators along the route, and a number of garages have helped to anchor offices in the area.

Providence, Rhode Island: The corner of Westminster Mall and Dorrance Street, where Westminster Street becomes a retail-oriented pedes-

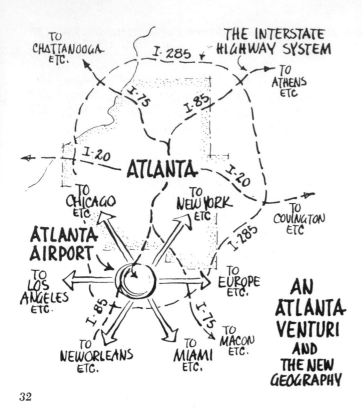

32

32, 33, 34, 35. *Upon closer examination, it turns out that the venturi principle offers a way of looking, not only at small traffic flows, but at regional and metropolitan concentrations of traffic. The tremendous flow of air traffic through Atlanta, of vehicular traffic through downtown El Paso, St. Petersburg, and Chicago, is partly an accident of geography, but reinforced by bridge and highway locations.*

33

EL PASO NATURAL VENTURI

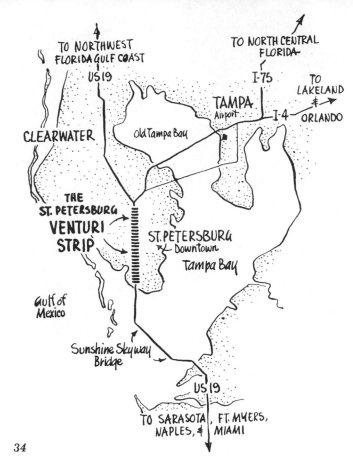

TO NORTHWEST
FLORIDA GULF COAST

TO NORTH CENTRAL
FLORIDA

US 19

I-75

TO
LAKELAND
&
ORLANDO

TAMPA
Airport

I-4

CLEARWATER

Old Tampa Bay

THE
ST. PETERSBURG
VENTURI
STRIP

ST. PETERSBURG
Downtown

Tampa Bay

Gulf of
Mexico

Sunshine Skyway
Bridge

US 19

TO SARASOTA, FT. MYERS,
NAPLES, & MIAMI

34

35

NEAR NORTH SIDE
RUSH ST.
OAK ST, ETC.

BEACH

LAKE SHORE DRIVE

JOHN
HANCOCK

LUXURY
APTS

LAKE
MICHIGAN

CHICAGO'S
MICHIGAN AVE.
BRIDGE
VENTURI

WATER
TOWER

SHOPS

MEDICAL
CENTER

WRIGLEY
BLDG

NEWS
PAPERS

NAVY
PIER

CHICAGO
RIVER

"ICRR
AIR RIGHTS"
AREA

RANDOLPH ST.

"THE LOOP"

STANDARD
OIL

SEARS
TOWER

FIRST
NATIONAL
BANK

LASALLE ST.

STATE ST.

MONROE ST.

MICHIGAN

ART
INSTITUTE

GRANT
PARK

36. Open since 1938 at this location, Carbone's Restaurant pulls drive-in trade from the Connecticut State Capitol, seats 85 with a 150 per cent turnover at midday, and is typical of many clubs and restaurants which pull downtown men away from old downtown sidewalk venturis.

trian mall, is an important venturi. Local men's clubs occupy top positions in nearby office buildings, although the prestigious University Club is several blocks away up College Hill on Benefit Street.

Savannah, Georgia: The vicinity of Johnson, Wright, and Chippewa squares provides this city's greatest mixture of hotels and clubs along Bull Street, the main north-south street, which connects the central core of old Savannah squares. The southern anchor of the Bull Street venturi is the Oglethorpe Club ("Members Only" sign), Union Army occupation headquarters after the Civil War.

Portland, Oregon, has an identifiable venturi around its central park blocks, partly because of the downtown location of the University, Arlington, and Multanomah clubs and the splendiferous Benson Hotel, all within easy walk of the Sixth and Broadway "heart." Downtown itself remains at relative high density.

Albany, New York: For nearly a decade, this capital city's downtown pathways have been disrupted by the removal of more than 3,000 dwellings to make way for the supercolossal South Mall, by the enforced suburbanization of state employees until the Mall is finished in the middle 1970's, and by giant renewal and highway projects. But the Fort Orange Club stands fast at 110 Washington Street, a block from the Capitol. As New York banks move onto State Street, as 16,000 displaced state em-

ployees move back downtown, and as new hotels arise on the Chapel
Street–Maiden Lane axis, some of the old foot traffic will resume. It appears likely that State and Eagle, at the lower crest of Capitol Hill, will
continue to be the major crossing for shoppers after political, financial,
and other goods.

The cargo value or informational load carried by each of these pathways is affected by the magnets, generators, and feeders[6] that contribute
to it; by the presence or absence of large office buildings and activity
centers (fig. 37); by the variety of public and private goings on in the
neighborhood; and by easy access and pleasures along the way—and
especially by competition from new media. There is no guarantee that
future cities will support traditional venturis as actively as in the past,
since the flow of electronic information via computers, private television
nets, conference calls, Confravision (the British television version of the
telephone conference call) is expanding by geometric leaps.

Today, many venturis carry lighter message-loads; those who walk

*37. Atlanta's prestigious Commerce Club, with its tiny promenade around
the top of the Commerce Building (foreground) near downtown Five Points
is an important watering place along the financial district's venturi. Peachtree
Center at top right. This view is northwest.*

these pathways are no longer seen as the real heavyweights (especially if you listen to old-timers "tell it like it used to be"). Country club living and spending habits have taken over, and many old-style downtown clubmen can no longer afford both. And new magnets arise in the suburbs. Clayton, Missouri, a bustling suburban county seat, with its restaurants and clubs, has become a noontime mecca for hundreds of St. Louis influentials who live around Clayton and pay high rents for office space. In the 1960's, they were paying higher rents for new offices in Clayton than they were for comparable space downtown. And they seldom hit their old haunts in downtown St. Louis. Power structures wax and wane, and thus it goes with their venturis.

No doubt there are many unmapped but well-known venturis in every city, awaiting discovery by outsiders. I would hope it will someday be as easy to get *these* maps as those at filling stations. Sidewalk action—like most beats—is visible, mappable, repeatable, and open to study by us all.

How does a stranger spot a venturi when he sees one? Not easily, for some indicators, such as clubs, are tucked out of sight; and the influential lawyer's office building may look like any other. One clue lies within the venturi itself—in the highly visible nature of conversations taking place along the sidewalk. Venturi operators group at doorways and corners, using the sidewalks as their stomping grounds. Old pols—the perennial knowledgeable, cynical, and affable politicians—tend to stand up against the nearest building, one leg thrust forward so they may pivot to right or left, depending on who is approaching, their heads and eyes sweeping the crowd. In flowing threesomes, and eddies of quartets, papers and briefcases at the ready, lawyers, executives, and such upper-level activists furnish the sidewalk action, contribute to its flow, and thus reveal its location to others.

Wherever men and women make important transactions, they require face-to-face gathering places where body English speaks and leads to consequences words alone can never generate. The venturi is the place where grouping, paper passing, arm twisting, lapel tugging, elbow grabbing, and physical threats or enticements—open or veiled—take place. And they work. Not even the clearest of electronic images, not even the fabulous holographic presences foreseen by Professor Dennis Gabor[7] and projected electronically around a conference table, can match the live and active physical presence that speaks so strongly in essential transactions.

Although some people insist they can learn to trust or distrust another person on television, I would argue that quite another, and more dependable, level of trust or avoidance is generated through repeated physical, visual, and verbal contacts of the sort that occur in the corridors, on the corners, across the new plazas, and through a city's Indian paths and informal meeting grounds. Table hopping at a luncheon club is no substitute for the more democratic mixing that occurs on the sidewalks. In one physical form or another, large and small versions of these essential venturis are likely to survive.

Made by Victor Gruen

To manufacture an image larger than life—a successful man-made epitome district—is a rare achievement, and we can learn much from the Fort Worth plan proposed in 1956 by the architect Victor Gruen.[8]

So successful was Gruen in selecting, simplifying, and then exaggerating the symptoms and solutions for a "dying downtown" that his plan captured the imaginations of central-city saviors across the land. His posture was defensive. The old city needed to be defended against its newest enemy, the automobile. Later, in his book, *The Heart of Our Cities*, he grew more explicit; it was necessary to set up "an inner defense line" plus "two further fortifications systems—to repel the invasion of mechanical hordes onto those areas where they create havoc."[9]

In the book, as in his public speeches, Gruen exhibited plans of medieval cities, including his native Vienna, bristling with walled forts, bounded by moats and fields of fire for defense. This was eloquent and powerful stuff to which downtowners responded in droves. Commissions for redoing downtowns poured in to the Gruen firm from all over: Fresno, Stamford, Paterson, Cincinnati, Manhattan, Rochester, Norfolk, Santa Monica, Vancouver, et al.

What Gruen had proposed at Fort Worth was a pedestrian-free core with beautiful malls, and around them an enclave of huge building blocks, reinforced by great parking garages at the corners, and the whole surrounded by a giant freeway system giving easy access to and from the heart (figs. 38 and 39). It was dramatic, grandiose, efficient—and expensive. Gruen's originality and verve, his ironic eloquence, put him into the national spotlight. His proposals were widely published; they became official doctrine in hundreds of city plans of the 1960's (fig. 40), and were built into the townscapes of the 1970's. If anything had become a major new epitome district of the American city by 1972, it was Gruen's.

Gruen thus came to stand for twentieth-century rational solutions to large-scale urban problems. His solutions were made up of large units, managed by large organizations, executed by big-scale finance and construction tactics—epitomizing the way twentieth-century American cities were heading. In contrast, the breaks we examined earlier represented the nineteenth-century mode of city expansion by means of a simplistic, repetitive gridiron pattern into which small operators, single-lot buyers, individual homeowners, and builders could fit. In a comparatively short time, from grid to Gruen, a major shift in scale had taken place.

38, 39. *How many versions of the 1956 Victor Gruen plan for downtown Fort Worth have been applied to American and other cities is unknown, but the dramatic simplicity of its elements has been widely copied: ring expressway, ramp garages to absorb incoming cars, and a pedestrian-free core.*

TOMORROW'S GREATER FORT W

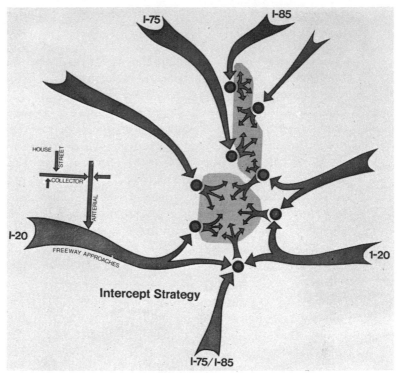

40. *Using defensive language from Gruen, who was using medieval images from Vienna, Atlanta planners set up an "intercept strategy" to soak up automobiles in parking facilities (dots) before they inundated the city core.*

The Identity-Makers

It became apparent to mayors, chambers of commerce, and local development promoters during the 1960's that local identity is capable of being converted into a money-maker in the new age of universal mobility.

As a result, epitome districts of a special sort have become a cliché, a gimmick whereby old identities may be refurbished and new ones fabricated as a device to promote the migration of industry and select population groups, especially tourists. Scores of cities now engage in fabulation—the art of fable-making—by assembling new versions of their former selves, spending fortunes on advertising to proclaim a new identity, and building structures and events to make that identity believable.

Seizing on old and well-known epitome districts, they balloon these into greater-than-life size and advertise them in national magazines. Atlanta proclaims itself to be "A New Kind of City," and capitalizes on its own blend of "Gone with the Wind" history and swinging in "Underground Atlanta." Indianapolis shortens its name on billboards to "Indy" to fit the racing image and newspaper headlines. There are dozens of self-styled "Cities on the Move" advertising their wares in business magazines and other media. Lacking other virtues to attract new growth, smaller cities brag about "Plenty of Room."

In this new age of myth-making, toponymy—the study of place names and their origins—has become a widespread obsession. Historical commissions get more power as cities seek to whip up their own historic districts. The Vieux Carre Commission of New Orleans, one of the oldest, uses its legal powers to coerce property owners into conforming to the proper architectural image. These powers have been firmly anchored to the Constitution by proving that the tourist-getting French Quarter image is important to the financial health and general welfare of the city.

No city considers itself sufficiently armed to entice foot-loose tourists or industrialists without a new sort of epitome district called Six Flags Over Ourtown, or Vacation Village, Frontierland, Pioneerland, Butchertown, German Village, Old(e) Town(e), or local imitations of Vieux Carre, Williamsburg, Sturbridge Village, Bavarian Alpine Village, and Old Salem.

These new epitome districts usually have most if not all the following indicators: a name; well-defined boundaries or a boundary zone; local history made evident in maps, pamphlets, etc.; a mythology; a central zone of action; gatekeepers or at least symbolic entrances; and a variety of signs and symbols. A significant indicator is an increase in neighborhood celebrations. New York City in three years increased the number of street-closing permits from some 700 to over 5,000 in 1972—mostly for neighborhood festivals. There is no limit to size: Disney World's 56,000 acres combined with its promoters' political power to collect highway interchanges and dominate the source of much of Florida's underground waters forecast a whole new scale of epitome districts which, under single managements, may become world meccas for tourism.

Travelers may discover themselves in a yet-to-be-defined epitome district through the presence of old place names, ethnic foods, religious carnival preparations; and become amateur historians by that simple device of trying to follow the old shore line in a waterfront city. ("There is Dock Street, we must be getting close.")

Surrounded by this mixture of newly emerging identity and old-style puffery, we need constant vigilance so as to match what we see happening against what is being artificially manufactured for us. Windbaggery —an airy form of packaging dear to chambers of commerce and tourism promoters—can easily blind us to the true nature of what is going on around us.

The "success" of any of these environments depends on a very special sort of exchange between it and us. The environment I call an epitome district must be information rich, and packed with visible evidence of complexities beyond itself. Each environment can be explained for and to us by signs, symbols, architectural manipulation, lighting, and other devices—explored with great ingenuity by Richard Wurman in *Making the*

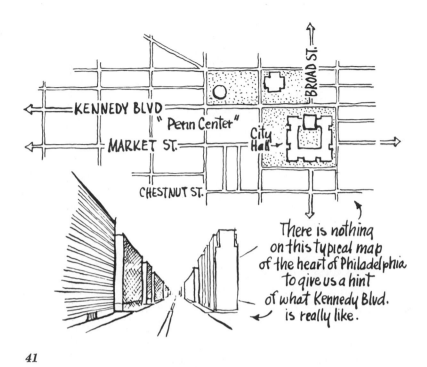

There is nothing on this typical map of the heart of Philadelphia to give us a hint of what Kennedy Blvd. is really like.

41

City Observable[10] and his other publications. But our survival depends on us, on our ability to see into any environment whether it is signed, lighted, mapped, explained or not (fig. 41). It is the *unmapped*, the *unadmitted* that we must cope with on our own. In all these shifty scenes, our survival depends on our ability to sense, and then to grasp, the environment's carrying capacity for existential meanings—meanings that only we can penetrate by participation in that scene, by our physical presence in, and movement through, it. Such scenes convey much; they imply even more. They have a high absorption capacity for receiving information, for projecting existential meanings, and for generating myths.[11]

Which means that we must bring something into these dealings with environments. It is *we* who can assign meanings to environments by using them and taking part in them, as Sister Annette Buttimer of the Clark University Graduate School of Geography has suggested.[12]

Thus epitome districts have the capacity to stir up responses in us. Such meanings get built up over time, and seldom flow to us all at once; it is the repeated coming back to a scene or place, perhaps over a lifetime, which adds to the layers of experience that we share with an environment. Thus when we find an epitome district we should treasure it, return whenever possible, and deliberately use it as a special indicator, not only of changes in the scene, but of changes in ourselves.

No such thing as the City or the Country remains. The former has penetrated the latter almost wholly, often invisibly but pervasively. Every United States Census counts the rise of population in that in-between land which is sometimes labeled "rural non-agricultural," and lies altogether within the network of a city's influence and its surpluses (fig. 42).

A city is a device for distributing surplus energy. While it performs many other functions, it carries out this one through a variety of channels including message systems, services, business connections, roads, pipelines, and wires. These networks undermine the political powers of country to resist city. They once transmitted powerful messages from country to city, but now carry streams of messages and energy unremittingly the other way. Neither city nor country can exist without the other—as New Yorkers occasionally learn to their dismay when a dock or truckers' strike stops the flow of food into that most fragile of cities. Yet cities, the surpluses they generate and the powers they coalesce, continue to dominate country in their search for markets to control and room to expand.

This region, which epitomizes dynamic unrest, I call the urban front, a place where phrases like "the edge of the city" have no contact with reality (fig. 43). A city's edge is where the action *was*, but is no longer (fig. 44). Often, as a journalist I have inspected what was locally described as "the edge of town" or "the beginning of real farming country." But even the most cursory investigation would reveal land to be held by

Fronts

speculators, not dirt farmers. The chief crop was capital gains, not cattle —extravagant fences being the first clue. That landscape was already dotted with fireplugs, transformers, public-hearing placards, and other urbanizing tackle; it was crisscrossed by a network of easements, future rights-of-way, utility lines and planned zoning changes, and extensions of the nearest urban energy source (figs. 45, 46, 47, and 48).

While debates may continue about how to identify and make legible the city and its edges, these will seem trivial in comparison with the larger forces at work and the problems to be solved on these fronts. The ancient image of walled cities with their visible, definable edges is dead (fig. 49). The European dream of a sharp and abrupt city-country division, with apartments on the city side, and open fields on the other, has no meaning here, except for rare instances such as military or Indian reservations (figs. 50 and 51).

42. This is how most Americans grapple with the American landscape—the first map of our "daily urban systems," based on commuting patterns of the 1960 Census. Most of the eastern and central states lie within these urban fields.

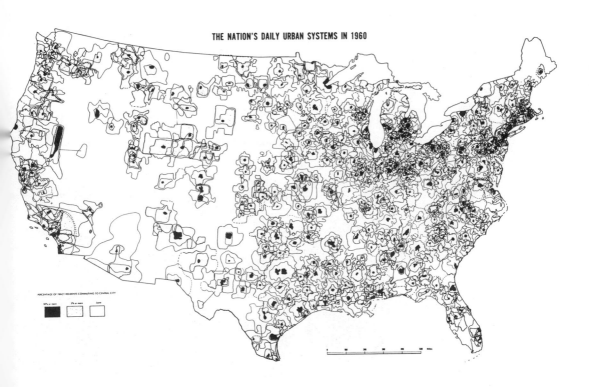

THE NATION'S DAILY URBAN SYSTEMS IN 1960

43. "Houston is not a city but a region, a form whose connections extend over distances inconceivable in traditional urban situations," observes Peter C. Papademetriou in the tradition-breaking AIA Guide to Houston (1972).

44. Overturned township marker on tributary to Narragansett Bay, Rhode Island, near Kingston.

45. *The tackle of urbanization: New man-made energies replacing the old agricultural scene at Columbia, Maryland: pipeline weld-ers' acetylene tank (foreground), prefab util-ity pole (rear), and sagging silo in abandoned farmstead constitute quick visual clues to what is happening as this site is fast con-verted for a newtown.*

46, 47, 48. *Trying on Milwaukee for size: More than thirty-two miles apart as the crow flies, the private airport west of Cedarburg, Wisconsin ("No Snowmobiles"), is part of the Milwaukee northern-front activity zone, while the garbage cans along the highway in Frank-lin Township thirty-three miles southwest in-dicate the spread of urban services into what looks like farming country. The "Don't talk" warning billboard fifteen miles outside Mil-waukee is another sort of indicator, concealing more than it reveals.*

47

46

48

49. *Tidy, neat, sharp edges of European cities such as The Hague are used to back up arguments that American cities, too, ought to have clean edges. But this only happens when land is extraordinarily scarce, and where strong government power forces land into prescribed uses. Photo, 1958.*

50, 51. *Rare example of a stabilized urban front: Pima Road forms the eastern boundary of Scottsdale, Arizona, with the Salt River Pima Indian Reservation on the right. Airview shows total buildup of subdivisions in the 1960's along west side of Pima Road. Photo of Indian youngster with tractor looks east across irrigated flatlands to distant Usery Mountains, in Tonto National Forest area.*

Dynamics of the Front

I use the term "front" in both its military (battlefront) sense and in its meteorological (weather front) context. Militarily, a front is simply a zone of armed conflict or stalemate. Meteorologists use the term to describe that "boundary which separates masses of air of unlike temperature, but is associated with no discontinuity of the pressure surface across it."[1] Although there are many other words that help one grapple with these matters—edge, ecotone, interface, boundary, fringe, margin, brink, threshold—the word front enables us to consider these place-processes as zones of unpredictable change, uneasy alliances and standoffs, and active citizen negotiation and treaty making (fig. 52).

Fronts are the dispersal zones for many goings on that were once anchored tightly to city land. Consider the sight of the Flea Market Shopping Center along Interstate 10, seven miles west of Jacksonville, Florida, built in 1971. Its very presence shows the owner's expectation that urban front-runners will be dumped at his doorstep via the new highway access. The same rationale underlies those "Condominium for Sale" signs in the semidesert far north of Fresno, California: a continuing redefinition of the size of the urban front.

52. *Different forms of marine life find their ecological niches in the intertidal area, or ecotone, of the Maine coast, much as mobile urbanites roam the urban fronts seeking their own proper, personal mixture of access, convenience, privacy, space, and expense. These are zones of interaction where energies are in constant flux.*

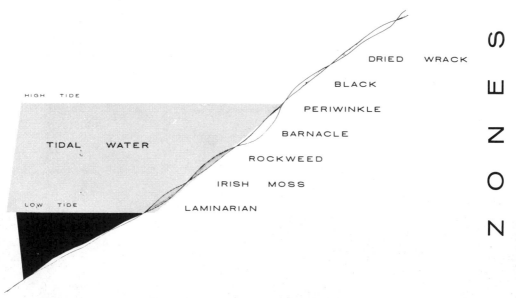

DRIED   WRACK

BLACK

PERIWINKLE

BARNACLE

ROCKWEED

IRISH   MOSS

LAMINARIAN

HIGH   TIDE

TIDAL   WATER

LOW   TIDE

Z O N E S

INTERTIDAL   AREA
(M A I N E   C O A S T)

53. *Denver: South Broadway near the Arapahoe/Elbert County line, 12 miles south of downtown Denver.*

54. *Located in the midst of two urban fronts, newtown Columbia, Maryland, has a major job center on its own industrial fringes—General Electric Company's Appliance Park East.*

55. *Erlanger, Kentucky: fast-building truck stop off Interstates 71/75 serving a fast-growth industrict south of Cincinnati. Left foreground: an in-transit prefab house module. Bottom: new dirt dumped for expanding the vast parking area.*

Most of the next 100 million people added to our population will inevitably be accommodated on these urban fronts. Given reasonable choices in housing types, they will continue to opt for old and new forms of suburbia. This is also where the jobs are moving (figs. 53, 54, and 55). During the 1960's the suburbs of fifteen major metropolitan areas gained 44 per cent more new jobs, while their central cities lost 7 per cent. In those same areas, the number of people who both live and work in suburbs increased 40 per cent.[2]

To recognize this great sorting-out process does not mean to turn one's back on the central city and its difficulties, but to put the older central city in its contemporary setting, a stage covering hundreds and often tens of thousands of square miles. It is a long way from the old City Hall.

Swarming

One could see the future coming most clearly on that summer weekend in 1969 when some 350,000 young people on their bikes, in campers, cars, trucks, and afoot clogged the highways and inundated the countryside in the Catskills of New York State: the beginning of the so-called Woodstock era when cars were packed bumper-to-bumper for thirty miles trying to get to the "great trip" that Woodstock promised and produced.

Such swarming is the coming together by impulse-determination of mobile communities—Woodstock, 1969, or Bull Island, Illinois, 1972. Swarming redefines community, prompts new consciousness and identity. And it will not go away, for it is created by a self-conscious, youthful society that possesses instant mobility, access to media, and its own, national word-of-mouth communication network.

Never before has United States society generated such a well-distributed capacity for crowd formation. One look at the expanding, commercial convention business will tell you that yesterday's limit is tomorrow's minimum. Never before the Woodstock festival had so many expectants assembled under such mixed primitive/festive conditions, which were peaceably replicated at Bull Island, Illinois. Drugs, both hard and soft, eased the pain of Woodstock's high density and hunger in the mud and rain—first evidence for millions of older outsiders that this form of mass experience and instant community was not to be sneered at or locked out. Clearly, something more pervasive than drugs was at work, then and later.

Swarming in nineteenth-century New England meant sending a colony from an established church out into the wilderness to form a mission. Some called it "hiving." Then and now, it arose from a search for community and empathy apart from old ways. It becomes an escape from establishment, a getaway from monopolies represented by old cities, an effort—strangely like those of typical suburbanites—to find a place to enjoy "before it gets all fucked up," in the various meanings of that term.

Swarming gives previews of new life styles on the urban front. It requires no building—only sites, accessibility, mobility, services, security, information, and a new view of the world.

Swarming puts a premium on swarmers' mobility and self-sufficiency. What established society has overlooked is that swarming is evidence of a new minority group declaring its identity. Since Woodstock, it has acquired its own prophet in Charles Reich (*The Greening of America*)[3] and others whose writings have formed a wave of significant, if erratic, journalism. If there were ever a case of identity formation, this was it.

Not all swarming was groovy, outdoorsy fun and games. Some swarmers got the "Easy Rider" reaction from ill-trained or rancorous deputies and redneck reactionaries. But short of the local perversions of vigilante movements, or of fascism taking over, there is no way swarming can be forced to a halt. The restless human energies are still there; the search for new community through mobility seems to pervade the entire society. And there is no way to disinvent mobility.

The Last Frontier Back

Geographic mobility is a special American thing; a mode of learning and getting with it; a means of personal advance, a way of making it. It implies, without guaranteeing, social mobility. Most Americans see their histories as migrational success stories—movement from the old country to new beginnings (fig. 56). History, American style, is seen as a series of confrontations between explorers and raw nature, between white settlers and red Indians, between open-rangers and homesteaders, claim stakers and fence jumpers.

The so-called end of the American frontier era can be pinpointed to the 1890 Census, when its superintendent summarized the results as follows:

> Up to and including 1880, the country had a frontier of settlement, but at present the unsettled area has been so broken into by isolated bodies of settlement that there can hardly be said to be a frontier line. In the discussion of its extent, its westward movement, etc., it cannot, therefore, any longer have a place in the census.[4]

Finis. Kaput. The end.

So stimulated by these findings was the young historian Frederick Jackson Turner that, in 1893, he wrote what has been considered one of

56

the most important single insights into the American character. He observed that:

> Up to our own day, American history has been in a large degree the history of the colonization of the Great West. The existence of an area of free land, its continuous recession, and the advance of American settlement westward, explain American development. . . . This perennial rebirth . . . this fluidity of American life, this expansion westward with its new opportunities, its continuous touch with the simplicity of primitive society, furnish the forces dominating American character.[5]

That frontier was defined as the margin of settlement which has a density of two or more settlers to the square mile, and also as the edge of free land.

Against this significant backdrop, I think it is useful now to ask what realm of American life is having a similar formative effect upon the American character. What is today's frontier? Does it, or can it, have any territorial or geographical identity?

What we are seeing today is a shift in the old frontier from an East-West polarity to the zones of metropolitan influence of urban fronts. One may watch nineteenth-century Western rituals re-enacted on television, but if it is the real thing you want, go to the urban fronts (fig. 57).

'Ranchers' Face 'Homesteaders' in Barrington Zoning Showdown

BY JERRY CRIMMINS

The ranchers and the homesteaders will be at it again tomorrow in a re-enactment of that great American drama, the range war.

Tomorrow's presentation will be shown at 3 p.m. in the Barrington Safety building, 121 S. Station st., Barrington.

In this updated version of the classic frontier feud, the range is approximately 473 acres in Barrington township. Substituting for the hackneyed "hired guns" will be retained attorneys. The moral lesson will be revealed later by the Cook County zoning board of appeals.

Winston Developers in Fray

Produced by the Winston Development corporation, the conflict up till now has been directed by the property owners of Barrington.

In the last episode, the homesteaders, played by the Winston Development corporation, came meekly to town to

dollars in assets. Muss showed considerable spunk ...

obscured when the motions start to fly, is based on the traditional values of wide open spaces.

Barrington's Republican state Sen. John A. Graham estimated that the homesteaders would flock into the development to the tune of 35,000 persons. This is aimed at 19 persons for every dwelling unit in the present Winston plans. The homesteaders would not be satisfied with the 473 acres, Graham predicted, after the last skirmish. They will eventually grow to take in all the surrounding unincorporated (not fenced in) area, he said.

Could Ruin Water

The residential development would also ruin the local water supply, Sen. Graham said, because of sewage.

Winston vice president Allan

While the ranchers braced ... upset this proposition, Muss was ...

Grossman vigorously disagreed and offered to show Sen. Graham how the water supply would be protected.

Paul M. Corbett, president of the Barrington Countryside association, said, "The people out here moved here to get away from all this." They like the sparsely settled uncrowded land, Corbett said.

The homesteaders on their part are offering to bring new amenities to the unsettled acres, such as a golf course, a man-made lake, to be called Winston lake, and a shopping center.

'Texas Oil' Controls

Corbett placed little stock that Winston homesteaders' eastern origins. They're controlled by Texas oil millionaires, Corbett said.

57. "The ranchers and the homesteaders will be at it again tomorrow in a re-enactment of that great American drama, the range war . . . the range is approximately 473 acres in Barrington [Ill.] township."—Chicago Tribune (March 8, 1970).

November 15, 1971 / 50 cents

Newsweek

58. New frontiersmen and women of the 1970's in a zone of contention that has moved from the Old West to the urban fronts around all expanding cities.

Weapons out there are not six-guns and fast cavalry but annexation ordinances, rights of incorporation, municipal housing policies, busing legislation, social and racial exclusionary practices, control over water lines, utility and tax rates, zoning, and police. Territorial rights are exercised not against red Indians but against city expanders and annexers, who are fought off by suburbanite lawsuits, with the help of anti-big-city state legislatures (fig. 58).

This is a useful way to look at current metropolitan development in the United States. On urban fronts, the language adopted by the contestants is that of the Old West; the images are historic. Land speculators clothe themselves in the language of frontiersmanship: I have heard them claim the right to "establish colonies . . . out where a man can enjoy the freedom of fresh air and a clean start." White suburbanites, resisting big-city public housing, racially mixed apartments, or annexations, assert that they (like the early frontiersmen) moved out here to get away from all those bad influences, and allege a right to exclude latecomers. And so history is perverted and freedom foreclosed on many an urban front, where the last one in wants to be the last to be admitted. Thus, the old frontier zone of guerrilla warfare now occupies a more or less circular front around all dynamic cities. It is to this front, and its evidence, that we now turn our attention.

Nature Fronts

On every dynamic urban front, there is a zone of action where the pastures run out and bulldozers run in, where field larks are replaced by Thunderbirds and Cougars in new garages, wells by pipes, fields by lawns, and soil by pavement. A landscape formerly dominated by natural forms and processes now gives way to the built environment. (When towns and cities diminish, the process reverses, nature takes over, grass grows in the streets, and woodland sprawl begins.)

To tell which way the battle is going—whether city expansion will continue to destroy country in the usual fashion—requires not only careful scrutiny, but some patience. Are developers still bulldozing down every tree in sight, ditching and straightening creeks, burying marshes, burning woodlands, laying waste to the millions of small niches, nests, burrows, warrens, hollows, dens, and watering places on which each small ecosystem depends? (See fig. 59.)

For answers, one may look at a dynamic waterfront such as an ocean resort (fig. 60), or at any restless local river front, the traditional battleground between the river's energies and those of the city people on its banks. Between floods, everything looks serene. But observe carefully the

The food-chain pyramid. Each level of creatures depends on those in the layers beneath it. Try drawing a food pyramid for man, and work out what would happen if one layer was destroyed

3
one large predator
(sparrowhawk)

2
a few small predators
(passerines)

1
many very small herbivores
(invertebrates)

abundant green leaves

59. *Ecology students at University of Waterloo, Ontario, uncovered a "hawk ring" around Toronto, twelve miles out. Landscape inside the ring is too heavily urbanized for wildlife to survive. Beyond the ring, farmers kill the hawks. The twelve-mile zone has just the wildlife balance to support hawks in this highly specialized front.*

60. *Highly competitive urban front: Miami Beach where hotel owners seek to grab scarce sand from a restless ocean. Most have given up and covered the old beach with patios, pools, cabanas, hoping that jetties will stabilize an essentially unstable environment.*

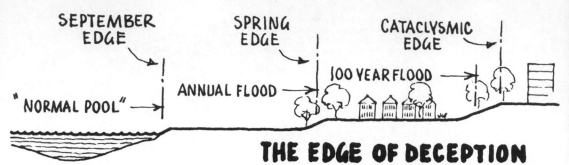

THE EDGE OF DECEPTION

*61. Another way of looking at waterfronts—as zones of centuries-long conten-
tion between man and nature where the scene is never the way it looks, but
always the way it might become, come hell and high waters.*

line where debris was deposited by the last flood. One may see innocu-
ous-looking streaks of yellow silt on the walls of houses, a white plastic
Clorox bottle jammed in a tree, brush lodged in a fence, or a line of bot-
tles along a valley's edge a mile back from the river's bank. This is an
instant clue to the river's true power to reach beyond its banks (fig. 61).

Walking the big-city waterfront, looking at the water's color, content,
and condition, one may see clearly that this front is subject to the conditions of the entire watershed. No one can "save" the local waterfront
merely by putting its legal control under a local waterfront commission,
since the sources of traffic, floods, pollution, and debris are all upstream.
River policy, therefore, derives from land policy, and not the other way
around.

Guerrilla Suburbia

Within each urban front lie subregions where the forces of city expansion
run strongest, where country is in full retreat. Since no American city has
the kind of political and monopolistic power that distinguished European
cities for hundreds of years, in its aggressive dealings with its neighbors
it must fall back on negotiation, persuasion, and various forms of semi-
concealed skulduggery to mask its expansive intentions. I call this zone
of action "guerrilla suburbia."

More than ever before, it is now possible suddenly to make a long leap,
far beyond the city's traditional edge, and set up urban outposts. Often
surreptitiously, city officials or private investors (and sometimes the
two in cahoots) will secure land options and conclude arrangements
whereby some giant new city-benefiting project—a reservoir, airport,
hospital complex, shopping center, military base, will become a reality
far outside the city limit, beyond the old definition of urban front. To
suburbanites or country residents, it appears as the city's Trojan Horse,

sneaked into their midst by the powerful enemy and quickly bristling with menacing strangers.

Such zones of contention are becoming more common, as many urban fronts extend themselves: along U.S. highways 40 and 25, and interstates 70 and 75 between Columbus-Springfield-Hamilton and Cincinnati, Ohio (fig. 62); the several parallel routes between greater Cleveland-Akron-Canton; along highways 183 and 303, and the newer tollway connecting longtime Texas rivals Dallas and Fort Worth, which buried old rivalries sufficiently to build between them the country's largest intercontinental airport in the early 1970's.

Between two cities close together (up to seventy miles), the attractions are magnetic, as evidenced by vehicle licenses, truck identities, and other signs (fig. 63). Cities along the whole eastern megalopolis, from Boston to Washington, exercise a strong linear pull, growing toward one another.

62. Geopolitics and city competition: in the struggle for southern Ohio markets, a Dayton advertising firm invents the term "megacity" to describe its trade/service region without even showing its much larger neighbor, Cincinnati, which dominates the region. Darkest shading indicates a heavily urbanized region from Columbus at upper right to northern Kentucky at bottom.

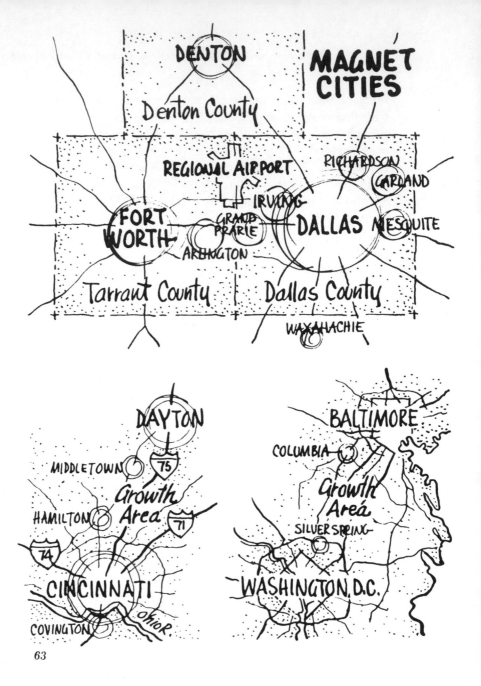

63

Two such magnet cities set up a zone of attraction and contention between themselves, usually shown most clearly along major highways. Here you will see taxis, buses, and service and delivery trucks from both magnets working the competition zone (fig. 64). Home builders and other contractors from one magnet extend their own radius to work the opposite pole; families from the Baltimore suburbs shop in outer Washington or at newtown Columbia, Maryland, whose residents may drive forty minutes in either direction to work, shop, or visit. In Minnesota, those onetime arm's-length and suspicious neighbors, Minneapolis and St. Paul, now share a sports stadium between them, and a visitor may observe traffic from both cities mixing and crossing along University Avenue and Interstate 94, which link the Twin Cities.[6] The in-between zone becomes highly competitive as soon as local service and sales firms from both directions obtain equal access to new customers.

The scale of all this is staggering. One land company has assembled more than 100,000 acres for lot sales in the region of El Paso, Texas;[7] major development firms in Florida have amassed hundreds of thousands of acres; the Alfred I. du Pont Estate, through control of the St. Joe Paper Company and the St. Joseph Land and Development Company, controls 100 miles of the Florida Panhandle Gulf coastline.[8] A striking phenomenon of the 1970's has been the continued purchase of giant tracts far from major cities especially on the seacoasts, for future development.

Increasingly, the guerrilla front is penetrated by these agents and front-runners so that economists who speak of the "urban-rural continuum" are describing a pressure zone of influence that extends far outward from one city only to meet a distant neighbor's zone at some midpoint. The planner Constantinos Doxiadis, in estimating the future growth of Detroit, has described how his staff, tracing the buying of land in

64. Increasingly the direction of urban growth is being manipulated by cities, counties and states eager to build up their tax revenues by urbanization. In this competitive tug of war, neighbors with only one traditional direction open for growth spend fantastic sums for bridges, mass transit or other devices to "get out of the box."

southern Michigan for purposes associated with the future growth of Detroit, discovered land being bought by speculators from Chicago, 275 miles to the west.[9]

Standing in such a zone—between two magnet cities—or on the interface between high and low densities, one is tempted to generalize. This is a scene that prompts pompous pronouncements. Anyone, for example, can grab a few census figures, sweep his eyes grandly across a suburban farm outside a city having high immigration and low unemployment, and pronounce eloquently "All these fields will be subdivided in the next ten years." But, of course, he will be wrong, and anyone who puts his money where his mouth is, talking like that, will go broke long before his generalization breaks down.

What separates the sheep from the goats is the capacity to be right a reasonable percentage of the time—correct in local, testable detail and not merely in loose generalization that can only be tested by large-scale mapping or computer techniques.

As it turns out, all fields do not get subdivided at the same rate because, as a matter of record, they are owned by many owners having different life styles and rates of attrition, credit, and patience—and also because some fields are repellent to the current generation of land speculators. They may look "ripe" but conceal subsoils resistant to septic tanks; or they reveal legal confusions dating back to the last Texas syndicate that bitched up the title after a run of dry wells and second mortgages.

Some places attract no traffic and lie vacant for reasons that appear to be no reasons at all. Some are "invisible," carrying social opprobrium, blighted by some historical event or functional quirk, as investors have learned to their regret. Locations just beyond, or just approaching certain traffic lights or other congestion points where a driver's attention is riveted to the road and not to the roadside, are notoriously bad places for certain drive-in businesses. Partly to offset this, many franchise drive-in businesses, in the 1960's, went into an architectural tizzy from which whole buildings emerged as signs so loud, high, bright, and visually persistent as to penetrate each driver's attention. Highway strips create miles of attention getters. Other spots become essential stopping places for tourists with predictably full bladders or empty gas tanks—a fact not apparent at a glance to outsiders.

Such hidden facts infuse all scenes. Intuition alone is never enough to explain what you see. One must learn to trust intuition but also to pursue its leads; to follow hints from peripheral vision but always to dig beyond first impressions; to see through a scene and its many processes, but also to see through it in time, to understand how it came to be, and to guess more skillfully at what it might become.

THE DIRTY OLD MAN of the urban scene is the highway strip. The dirty word in the urban lexicon is "to strip." Strips "pose the most difficult and serious land use problems facing the city," says the Denver comprehensive plan for 1985. A strip is "a miserable place for the shopper to buy and the merchant to sell . . . a drain on the city," says a widely published, 1969 University of Tennessee study.[1] It is "one long rip-off," observes a student when we meet at Oklahoma State University;[2] "a static linear city," says Christopher Tunnard in *The City of Man*,[3] "a massive elongated bloodclot," says a Rhode Island study.[4]

In short, the strip is the urban/suburban scapegoat. Demonstrating its iniquity became a major preoccupation in the 1960's among aesthetic *arrivistes* who looked at it critically and distorted it photographically with telephoto lens, usually for propaganda purposes. If you have seen one of those photos, you have seen them all. The strip became the battleground for class-judgment makers, which explains the high emotional pitch of frenetic suburban zoning, or antizoning, public hearings. But it does not tell us what, besides an object of scorn, we are to make of strips. (See figs. 65 and 66.)

The question remains: "What goes on out there?" Once we ask and begin looking carefully at strips and at the social forces thereby revealed, we are bound to see significant patterns. All strips are by no means alike. Some specialize and thus give us clues to the neighborhoods they serve.

Strips

New forms are developing, old ones decaying. Here the essence of urban forces is revealed, if we will only look open-eyed and open-minded.

The strip is easy to find, quickly defined, often carries a familiar name such as Sunset Strip, and projects strong images and emotional memories as an identity district. Most people who move about their own communities are able to identify not one but many strips. Teenagers of driving age are vastly knowledgeable about the pecking order of strips—where cops hang out in unmarked cars, where the drag racers gather after midnight, which drive-in zone is frequented by which high-school crowd —i.e., what functions they perform and how well or badly they do so.

65, 66. If you get it, you spend it. This rule of life for millions of Americans makes possible thousands of miles of commercial strips, such as these in Spokane and Baltimore (opposite), where major proportions of retail sales and service take place.

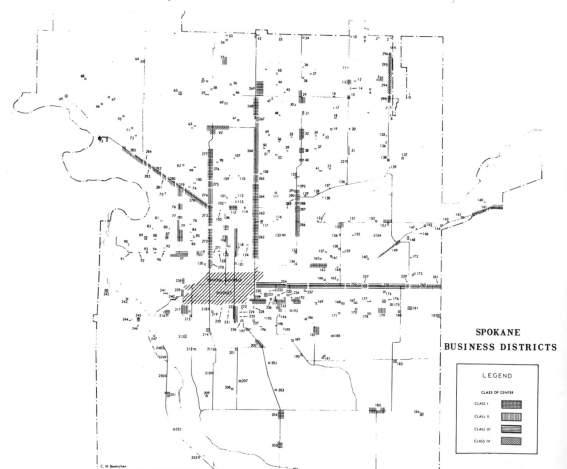

SPOKANE
BUSINESS DISTRICTS

LEGEND

CLASS OF CENTER

CLASS I
CLASS II
CLASS III
CLASS IV

C. W. Beatschan

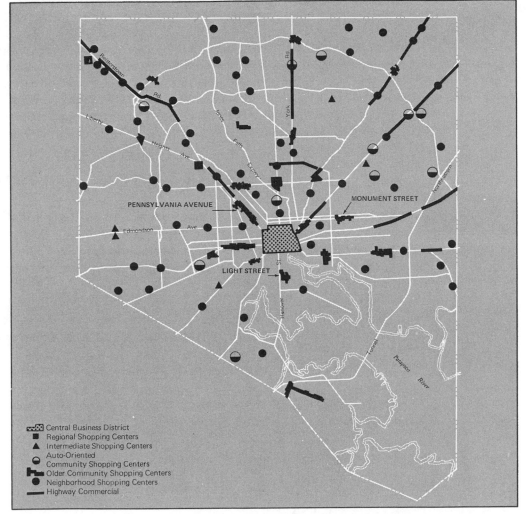

PENNSYLVANIA AVENUE

MONUMENT STREET

LIGHT STREET

- ▦ Central Business District
- ■ Regional Shopping Centers
- ▲ Intermediate Shopping Centers
- ◓ Auto-Oriented
  Community Shopping Centers
- ┣┳ Older Community Shopping Centers
- ● Neighborhood Shopping Centers
- ▬ Highway Commercial

The Roadside Surplus Disposal Area

Earlier, I described the city as a device for distributing surplus energies, for it is a commonplace to note that cities throw off surpluses of population, products, services, and wastes. So long as the North American economy continues to grow, well into the twenty-first century, the highway strip is likely to continue serving a vital function as a linear disposal area for surplus urban energies. As surpluses change, strips will react.

On the strip, automobility runs rampant, carrying that valuable cargo called "accessibility" to be dropped off anywhere along the way. The efficient strip is the path of least resistance. On the strip, one can set up shop in a hurry, dispose of a cargo to dozens of buyers, move in or move out quickly, and deal in short haggles. It is a place of easy transactions. If you do not like it, try down the road.

Rules on the strip are less strict than those downtown or in older, denser commercial zones. The newer the strip, the fewer immediate neighbors there are to be affected by noise, light, and other activities. As strips age, they are repaired piecemeal. There is a constant coming and going; population turnover is high. To expect stability of a strip is to misunderstand its very nature.

Where It All Started: River Strips

The earliest strips to be found are in river valleys, those ruts of civilization, pathways of early settlers the world over. To pinpoint a river strip should be easy for travelers anywhere in North America (fig. 67).

Stop your vehicle if you are anywhere within sight of a river, natural lake, or ocean and look toward the water. Almost inevitably the ground slants toward water, and the earliest strip grew up along an old path or track at the top of the bank. Many such early strips were flooded out and moved to higher ground (fig. 68). Most river roads and coastal highways

67. *From coast to coast, this strip pattern has evolved: the old river road, often flooded; the new road built in the 1920's on higher ground; and finally the interstate, disregarding rough terrain, soaring across hill and dale.*

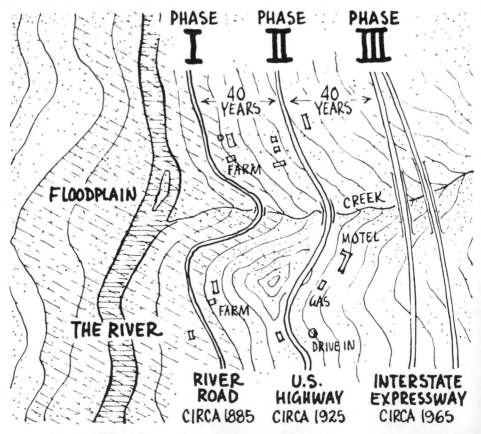

PHASE **I**   PHASE **II**   PHASE **III**

← 40 YEARS → ← 40 YEARS →

FARM

FLOODPLAIN   CREEK

MOTEL

FARM   GAS

THE RIVER   DRIVE IN

RIVER ROAD CIRCA 1885   U.S. HIGHWAY CIRCA 1925   INTERSTATE EXPRESSWAY CIRCA 1965

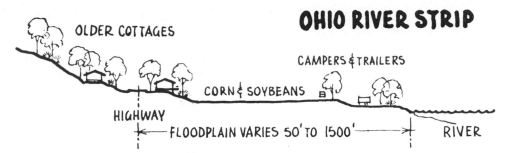

OLDER COTTAGES

CAMPERS & TRAILERS

CORN & SOYBEANS

HIGHWAY

FLOODPLAIN VARIES 50' TO 1500'

RIVER

68. *Strip-cropping has new meaning along major river systems as the old riverbank, often the site of early trails and roads, is taken over by seasonal residents, and the old highway gets lined with cottages. The next strip, when it arrives, will be uphill to the left.*

thus run in pairs with remnants of the older one closer to water. Often enough, the first railroads moved in between; both the railroads and the bigger highways that came later were products of larger energy systems at work—taxes and other subsidies of state and national government.

At every stage for some 150 years, bigger investments poured into new highway strips, generally on higher-ground sites (figs. 69 and 70). As American society grew more high-and-dry minded, it put its big investments out of the reach of floods and hurricanes—either far from the river bank or on huge dikes and fills along the river itself—such as Interstate 91 along the Connecticut River, or Interstate 787 which pre-empts the river front of Albany, New York, or Interstates 71 and 64, respectively, bestowing the same disfavors on Cincinnati and Louisville.

69. *Early western strip grew up along banks of irrigation ditch, El Rancho, New Mexico, with later roads following the old settlement pattern along the waterside.*

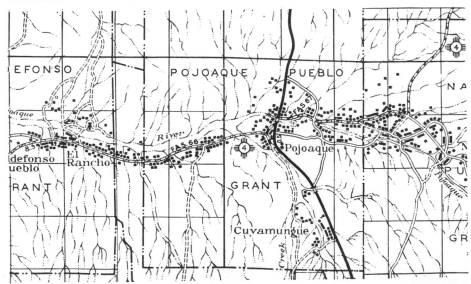

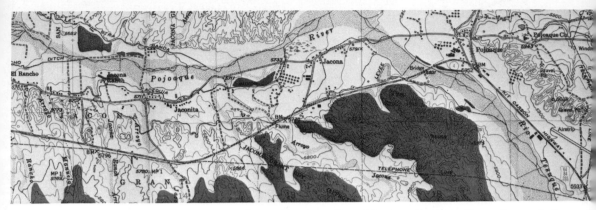

70. *A 1953 map of El Rancho area, New Mexico, shows early settlement along irrigation ditches in valley, with older strips following the water, while contemporary highway, a later high-energy-input construction job, has moved in uphill. They form typical downhill-uphill pair.*

Thus, many an original, low-lying river road tends today to be a strip of second-rate activities that cannot pay the price of land close to town—junk dealing, cheap storage, shacktowns, and small industries which survive flooding.

To look at river strips in this way enables us to judge all strips as products of their times, reflecting the amount of each generation's surplus energies which were available for investment in trafficways and automobility. At every stage things got bigger. How long this can continue is open to debate, but it is quite certain that strips will continue to be a major exhibition ground for which way the debate is going.

The Natural History of the Strip

Behind the so-called clutter of the strip lies a set of patterns, which discloses the natural history of the strip (fig. 71). At each stage, the strip puts on a separate act, and before one decides what ought to be done about a strip, it is essential to first discover what stage it is at in the recurring cycle of energy investment and decay. For some strips are ripe for change and others are not; still others may revert to an earlier phase.

In the beginning there was Strip I (fig. 72), and so primitive and persistent is its form that in many parts of North America it is still in use—and new ones are still being carved out of the landscape. Strip I often followed Indian or ancient animal paths and traces, a narrow dirt track winding along a stream, valley edge, or ridge top. Its job was to provide

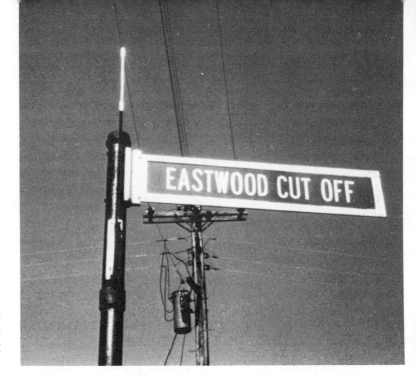

71. Where the natural history of the strip was discovered: at Eastwood Cut Off, Jefferson County, Kentucky, a second paved road downhill from earlier strip, uphill from the big new cut-and-fill strip.

access to one's place of work in field or forest, protection at a nearby fort, or a neighbor. Thousands of miles of still existing Strip-I routes within city and countryside may be discovered by any traveler.

Strip II (fig. 73) is usually, and simply, a wider version of Strip I, following the same route, but gradually improved for wagons until the coming of the automobile, sometimes becoming a linear village.

When automobiles came, so did Strip III (fig. 74). This was an early bypass, usually inserted along the back lot line of houses fronting onto Strips I and II. Many Strip III's were built in the 1920's as early paved roads. The character of Strip III varied from region to region. A New England Strip III might have been a mere kink in the road, but expanded in the Midwest to a larger scale.

The 1930's and 1940's ushered in heavier road-building equipment which carved out wider and deeper cut-and-fills through formerly inaccessible pathways. Highways took big parcels, no longer narrow tracts, and thus produced the next stage, or Strip IV (fig. 75), offering previews of the giant interstate routes a decade later. Highways became the biggest things around.

Next came Strip V (fig. 76), a product of the great road-widening era, in which old streets and highways were simply pushed out into the roadsides; lanes were added, roadsides reorganized, and new architectural forms developed. Left behind were thousands of houses and buildings, now truncated, defrocked, perched awkwardly (figs. 78, 79, 80, 81, and 82). This produced that familiar phenomenon, a multi-laned instrument of mixed access (fig. 83), and often a dangerous road to drive.

Familiar products of highway widenings—houses left in awkward attitudes and relations.

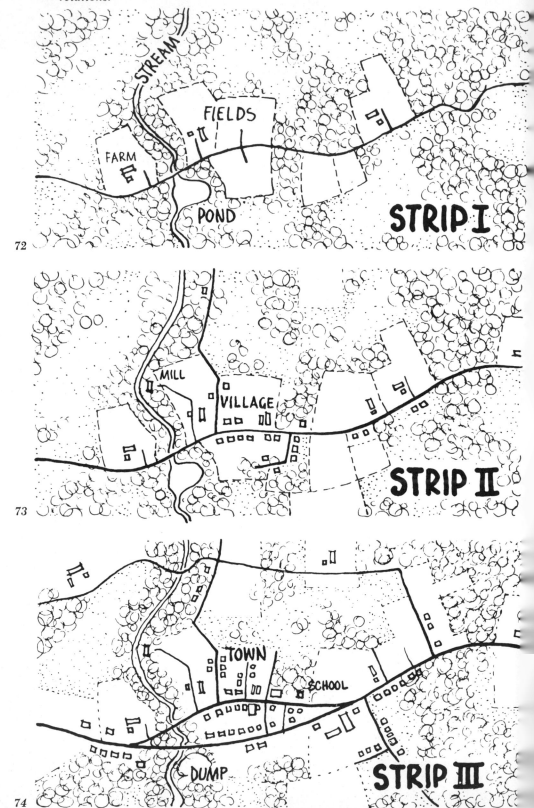

STREAM

FIELDS

FARM

POND

STRIP I

72

MILL

VILLAGE

STRIP II

73

TOWN

SCHOOL

DUMP

STRIP III

74

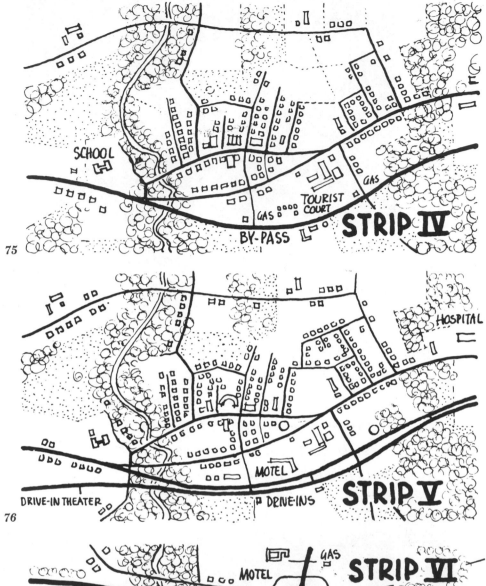

SCHOOL

GAS

TOURIST
COURT

GAS

GAS

BY-PASS

STRIP IV

75

HOSPITAL

MOTEL

DRIVE-IN THEATER

DRIVE-INS

STRIP V

76

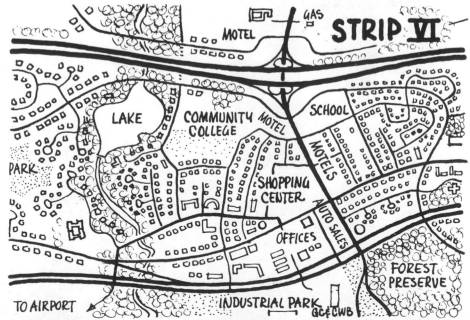

MOTEL

GAS

STRIP VI

LAKE

COMMUNITY
COLLEGE

MOTEL

SCHOOL

PARK

MOTELS

SHOPPING
CENTER

AUTO SALES

OFFICES

FOREST
PRESERVE

77   TO AIRPORT

INDUSTRIAL PARK

GC&CWB

78. *Darien, Connecticut, on U.S. 1.*

79. *South of Baltimore, Maryland, on Highway 176.*

80. *Delmarva Peninsula north of Norfolk, Virginia.*

81. *Starke, Florida, Highway 301 widened in 1963.*

82. *Gravois Road, St. Louis, Missouri.*

80

81

82

83. *What is left behind after a major highway cutting is a two-level town such as Elk Park, North Carolina. The old stores, post office, etc., were strung out along an early road, right, until highway was cut into hillside. What you see here are Strips I, II, and III in one view.*

84. *If you continue to see the same sign for a hundred miles, with different names, it indicates a major highway relocation. This is four-lane Highway 13 running north-south down the Delmarva (Delaware-Maryland-Virginia) Peninsula*

Strip VI (fig. 77) tends to develop at right angles to the older strips, along the access roads joining the older strips to new interstate interchanges, and here you find variations of "Motel Row," "Drive-in Gulch," or "Gasoline Alley."

Finally, Strip VII is a radical reorganization of nearly everything within the influence of the interstate interchange (fig. 84), encouraging heavy injections of "foreign" energy into the vicinity. An interchange zone is a real-estate merchandising device manufactured with public funds; it is an economic cockpit where only the largest operators can afford to compete—oil and motel chains, national land developers, newtown promoters. Highway policy promotes bigness, and most proposals for "cleaning up the strip" turn into devices for getting it into the hands of fewer, richer private owners, or under control of large governmental agencies. (See figs. 85, 86, and 87).

85. Recapture: after being bypassed by Highway 13, in 1967, the town of Onley, Virginia, reached out, annexed the new highway, doubled its area, and now advertises itself as "The Home of Economic Development."

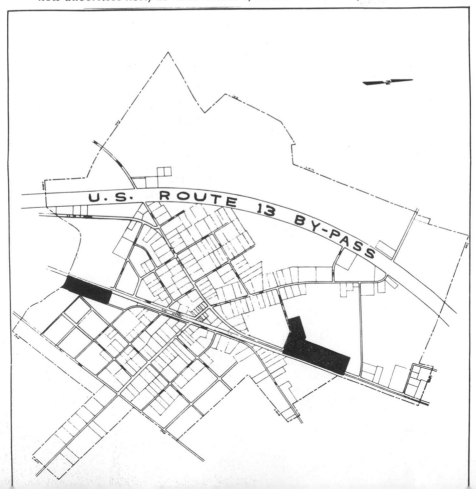

86. *Early paved-road remnants show (bottom right), while later Dixie High-way (upper right) was built on earth fill to raise it out of the flood plain of the Driftwood and White rivers. Clear case of downgrading properties along older strip: note half-buried garage. Southern Indiana.*

87. *Making the best of both strips, this homeowner near Lancaster, Ohio, now has two "fronts," one facing the older strip in distance, and well-clipped lawn fronting on limited-access Strip IV. Note metal deer facing the newer strip.*

How strips are to be reorganized is politically dynamic, since new interchange districts with self-governing powers can offer opportunities for financial and political enterprisers, unless they too are taken over by large-scale monopolists.

The Origins of Spotty Development

That old cut-and-fill process of digging through hills for dirt and rock to build up a roadbed across low spots is itself the cause of a plague afflicting most strips: "spotty development." Highway designers attempt to balance cut-and-fills to keep down the costs, but this makes spotty development inevitable where roads cross irregular terrain, as in most of North America (fig. 88).

Note that the crucial juncture is influencing future development where the slope of the land meets the level of the road. This is the only easy place you can get off the road onto the land, and return. I call it the topo-break. This is the first point at which roadside development takes place—where somebody can get on and off the road on an even keel.

For a clear view of spotty development caught in the act, look at Mt. Horeb, Wisconsin, between Madison and northern Iowa. Highway 18–

88. Cut-and-fill highway construction in the act of encouraging future spotty development: North Carolina Highway 19-E, between Spruce Pine and Crabtree, 1972. Surplus dirt from huge cuts is dumped as close to the cut as possible, setting up sites for future buildings.

89. Gonstead Clinic of Chiropractic (upper left) and its own motel occupy hilltop just outside Mt. Horeb, Wisconsin, with other hilltops occupied by driving range, implement dealer, etc.—while swales in between are vacant.

151, just outside Mt. Horeb, is a typical cut-and-fill product of a high-energy system; it cuts directly through the rolling terrain east of town to set up a landscape of castles on the hill, a dot-dash succession of car-truck dealers, chiropractors' offices, motel, and golf course, each perched atop its own knoll, with deep swales in between (fig. 89). Although Mt. Horeb is a growing touristic town, the energy is not there yet to fill in the ravines between those hilltop nodes. The result is classic of spotty development, an emerging strip at its most wasteful stage, forcing everyone to drive a hundred yards farther to the next node. Before it can change, the old cut-and-fill methods must be drastically modified to encourage unified development.

Pit-Stop America

There was a time when many city or suburban highway strips could be explained by saying they merely followed or ratified old commuting train or streetcar routes radiating from the city core. But the development of nonradial strips in hundreds of communities has shown that another dynamic is at work.

At some point in its life—usually when the strip becomes part of a highway network or web serving a region and not merely connecting two activity nodes—the strip becomes specialized as a pit stop for special markets (fig. 90). Strips which happen to be one day's drive from Chicago, Denver, or other travel generators quickly turn into motel strips as soon as interstate connections make the drive possible (fig. 91). Highway roadsides turn into long repair-sales strips for the region, as is the case outside Eugene, Oregon, where loggers' equipment for sale or trade lines the highway (fig. 92); and along Airline Highway between New Orleans and its airport—a strip for swamp buggies and oil drillers' equipment.

90. Nine miles of auto-directed businesses along southeast 82nd Avenue in Portland, Oregon, offer everything from food and drink at the Pit Stop Tavern to mobile offices next door and thousands of trailers, camper rigs, and trailer hitch repairmen.

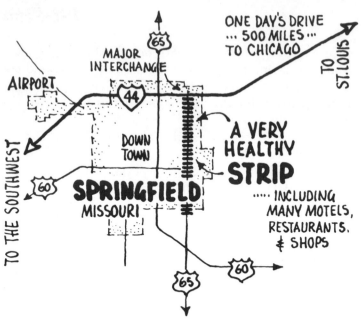

91. *Defying the old wagon-wheel image of a city's radial highway strips, many strips now flourish along outskirts axes near interstate interchanges, such as this variation.*

93. *The Hungry Mile of West Lindsey, Norman, Oklahoma, is a byproduct of the university's doubling in size in a decade, of complex zoning pressures, and the fast-food franchising boom which peaked in 1970. Result—restless rows of eating joints.*

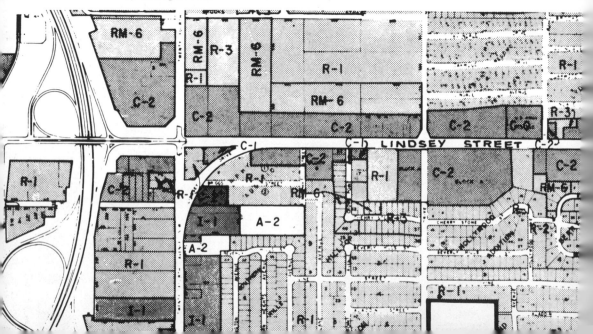

92. *Like leaping greyhounds or praying mantises, these big logging rigs line the highway outside Eugene, Oregon, within sight of forested mountains nearby. This is one of many pit stops catering to logging crews in Pacific Northwest.*

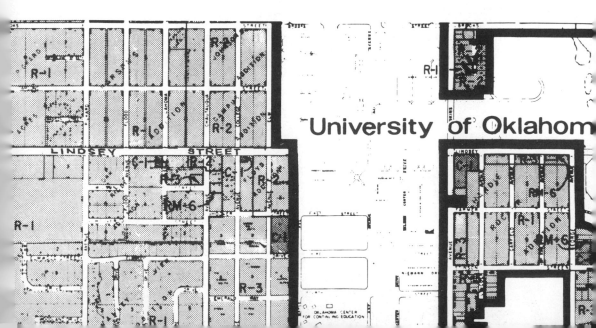

94. *Quick-stop sex. Small sign under marquee advertises "topless masseuses." One of many new highway and suburban porno-shops, this one in Southern Indiana has its outdoor movie lot screened (right, rear) so passersby cannot peek at X-rated movies.*

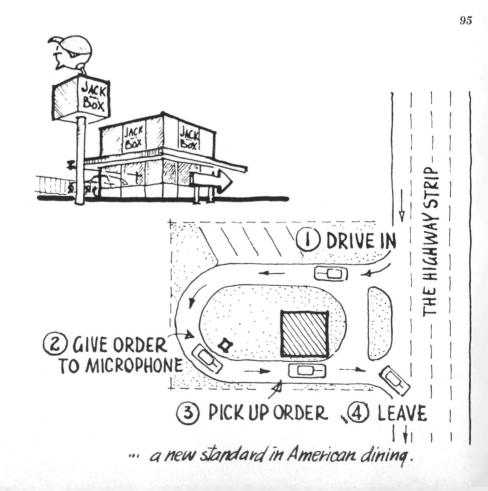

... *a new standard in American dining.*

95, 96, 97. *Jack-in-the-Box carries the quick-stop cram session to a 1972 conclusion in this multiple food-franchise drive-in corral on Morse Road, Columbus, Ohio, providing a haven for ten franchise feeders with joint parking around periphery and a common pool-patio in middle. Example of continued clustering.*

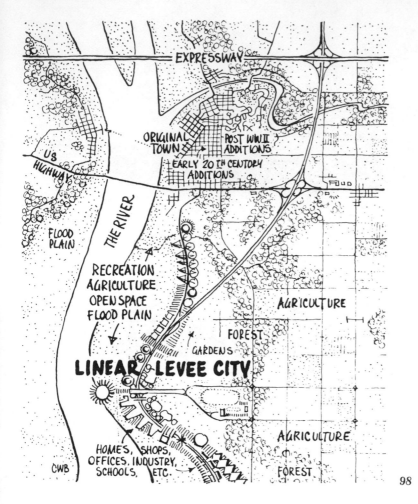

EXPRESSWAY

US HIGHWAY

ORIGINAL TOWN

POST WWII ADDITIONS

EARLY 20TH CENTURY ADDITIONS

FLOOD PLAIN

THE RIVER

RECREATION
AGRICULTURE
OPEN SPACE
FLOOD PLAIN

AGRICULTURE

FOREST
GARDENS

LINEAR LEVEE CITY

AGRICULTURE

FOREST

HOMES, SHOPS, OFFICES, INDUSTRY, SCHOOLS, ETC.

CWB

98

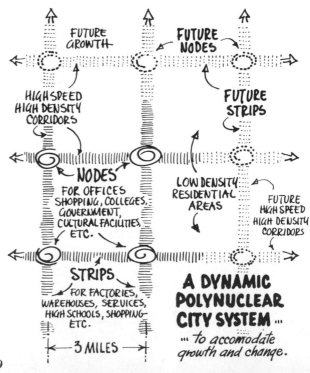

FUTURE GROWTH

FUTURE NODES

HIGH SPEED HIGH DENSITY CORRIDORS

FUTURE STRIPS

NODES
FOR OFFICES
SHOPPING, COLLEGES,
GOVERNMENT,
CULTURAL FACILITIES,
ETC.

LOW DENSITY RESIDENTIAL AREAS

FUTURE HIGH SPEED HIGH DENSITY CORRIDORS

STRIPS
FOR FACTORIES,
WAREHOUSES, SERVICES,
HIGH SCHOOLS, SHOPPING
ETC.

A DYNAMIC POLYNUCLEAR CITY SYSTEM ...
... to accomodate growth and change.

|← 3 MILES →|

98, 99, 100. Ways to go: These three sketches indicate how forces presently at work in Strips VI–VII may turn out. Some may use the Jefferson grid, getting reorganized into clusters or nodes at the intersections; or string along existing highways, settling down into specialized districts. Or they take advantage of the single-purpose flood-control levees of the U.S. Corps of Engineers, using them as linear building sites. What is most unlikely is that strips will disappear.

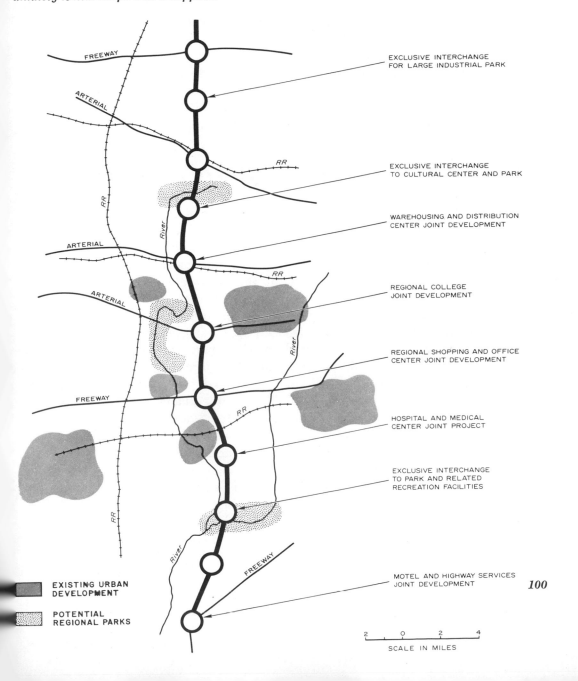

EXCLUSIVE INTERCHANGE
FOR LARGE INDUSTRIAL PARK

EXCLUSIVE INTERCHANGE
TO CULTURAL CENTER AND PARK

WAREHOUSING AND DISTRIBUTION
CENTER JOINT DEVELOPMENT

REGIONAL COLLEGE
JOINT DEVELOPMENT

REGIONAL SHOPPING AND OFFICE
CENTER JOINT DEVELOPMENT

HOSPITAL AND MEDICAL
CENTER JOINT PROJECT

EXCLUSIVE INTERCHANGE
TO PARK AND RELATED
RECREATION FACILITIES

MOTEL AND HIGHWAY SERVICES
JOINT DEVELOPMENT

100

EXISTING URBAN
DEVELOPMENT

POTENTIAL
REGIONAL PARKS

FREEWAY
ARTERIAL
RR
RR
River
ARTERIAL
RR
ARTERIAL
River
FREEWAY
RR
RR
River
FREEWAY

2   0   2   4
SCALE IN MILES

West of Norman, Oklahoma, the Hungry Mile of West Lindsey grew up during the fast-foods franchising boom of the 1960's between a new interchange and the University of Oklahoma—a multiple pit stop only five minutes' drive from thousands of hungry students (fig. 93). These linear pit strips serve the highway just as vitally as do the racing car pits at Indianapolis Speedway, LeMans, or Sebring. (See figs. 94, 95, 96, and 97.)

Even more specialized as a pit strip is Mission Road, just east of downtown Los Angeles. It has become the site of a remarkable auto-wreckers' strip, lined with salvage, repair, and spare-parts shops covering hundreds of acres. Why here? Because much of the land was owned by railroads, zoned for industry, had been filled in, and could not support large buildings. More than all this, it was easily accessible to that huge wreck-producing monster called the Los Angeles freeway system—and is now a vital stop at the end of the road. Thus the pits spin out their own explanations of the larger networks which they serve.

The Strip Is Trying to Tell Us Something

The strip is trying to tell us something about ourselves: namely, that most Americans prefer convenience; are determined to simplify as much of the mechanical, service, and distribution side of life as possible; and are willing to patronize and subsidize any informal, geographic behavior setting that helps. The value systems of the strip derive from the open road rather than from the closed city. Strips become the city's vital contact zones with surrounding regions, and their fast changes reflect population and taste shifts on the urban fronts. (See figs. 98, 99, and 100.)

You will note that, especially in describing Strip I, I stressed the influence of geographic environment which forced people to obey natural laws: do not build where you get flooded, work with and not against natural processes, use gravity and local, rather than imported, energy.

For several generations now, the United States has been on an energy binge, squandering capital resources while thinking of them as God-given, perpetual surpluses. The era that produced Strips IV–VII, from the 1920's through today, has led too many of us to think of energy as inexhaustible, that saving was old-fashioned, and plenty our birthright. This belief deluded us into the simplistic and unrealistic view that we could locate any activity wherever it pleased us. It has made us forget the constraints which surround every decision to do something *here* rather than *there*. It encourages us to overlook the fact that every locational choice is a balancing act in which we counterpoise and compare our available time, energy, money, material, machines, and the distances and sites over which they all must be deployed. In an affluent era we tend to overlook here-versus-there costs or to minimize their influence. But they still remain. Every day these decisions become more crucial, and as energy grows more expensive—gasoline at $2 per gallon, for example—we will reconsider our every move and mode.

Strip dwellers must choose sooner than most of us whether to go or stay, to lease or buy, where to move, how to survive in shifting scenes. They already know what most of us must still learn—that the necessity to choose between here and there will become a pressing daily concern, influencing our every glance and movement into the world beyond our door.

To MOVE or not to move; that is the question. To decide whether to make a move is, now more than ever before, a crucial daily issue for millions of Americans. Not for nothing are they described as "the world's movingest people." By 1969 they were traveling in passenger cars 1.5 times more than in 1959, and by air 3.5 times as far in 1970 as in 1960.[1] Their vehicles increased from about 60 million in 1959 to some 90 million in 1969 (fig. 101).[2] And they change their residences more often every year.

Yet where is move-making taught as a special subject in school? Do we take that new job, transfer to another town, try a new resort or drive-in, sell the old house, rent another flat, find a better bus, pick another commuting route, choose the sunny side of the street, stay off the interstate? Decisions, decisions, decisions . . .

The moment we move, we acquire other names and become newcomers, strangers, migrants, tourists, commuters, hustlers, surveyors, inspectors, deliverymen, runners, couriers, postmen, contact persons, scouts, agents, and traveling salesmen. As tourists, paraders, or travelers we may shed one self for another and turn into spendthrifts, lechers, or litterbugs: "There is no shame when you travel," goes an old Japanese saying. Once we quit moving and get back indoors we become different people with other titles: a route man stuck in the office is an anachronism.

The unifying link in this is the way we make environments work for us as behavior settings for regular, periodic, recurring movements. These I

Beats

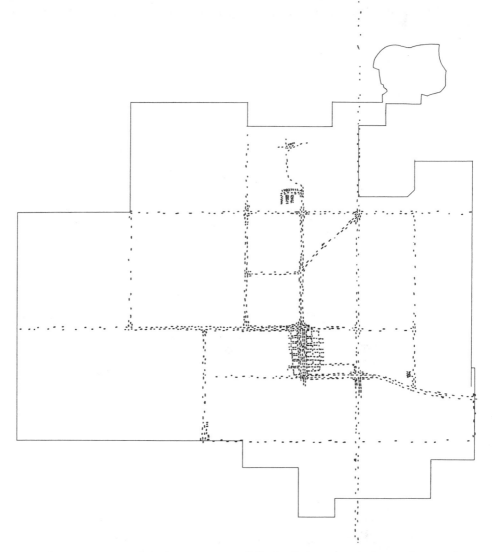

101. *"Moving around it in an automobile is the most persistent impression that Clovis [New Mexico] residents have of their city," reported Windell Kilmer and Mark Miller (New Mexico Quarterly, Fall, 1968). Three out of four students have cars, and local radio station refers to the "City on Wheels." Dashes on map show vehicular activity.*

call "beats," but they can also be defined as runs, trips, swings, or commutes which follow circuits, orbits, paths, rounds, and courses. Or they may be just the same old treadmill. Some beats are forays and retreats which involve regular encounters with environments outside our home range. Others, more irregular, are called sprees, frolics, toots, and larks. Nobody ever went on a spree, frolic, toot, or lark that was worth a damn while standing stock still.

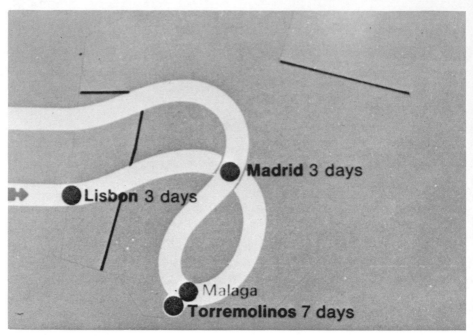

Because beats are cyclical and regular, they serve to organize human movements in and around cities and offer visible clues to cities' functional lives. Beats are predictable, mappable, and often negotiable. They can become quite valuable. If I can convince my banker that my property will become part of the beat of 30,000 tourists per day, he may lend me $200,000 to build a motel, provided nobody else gets there first. In fact, one of the distinguishing marks of the new beat is that it can be packaged, mass-produced, and merchandised. The "package deal" vacation may be bought from a travel agency, from a bank, or by mail, and the American Express Company has exploited packaging to the hilt with its bargain "swinger" vacations (fifteen to twenty-two days in Europe for Americans at $439 to $789). (See fig. 102.) The volume of such packaged vacations, voyages, outings, and trips is on the rise, often at reduced prices for anyone willing to be packaged for mass mobility.[3]

Beats have scope and scale, they come long and short, safe or chancey. Some, as illustrated here, consist of predictable upper-level encounters with a limited cross section of safe little worlds (fig. 103). Other beats cut through all social classes (fig. 104), exposing one to risks and opportunities. With a bit of work, any beat may be mapped and computerized. Police in Chicago and elsewhere computerize their beats in order

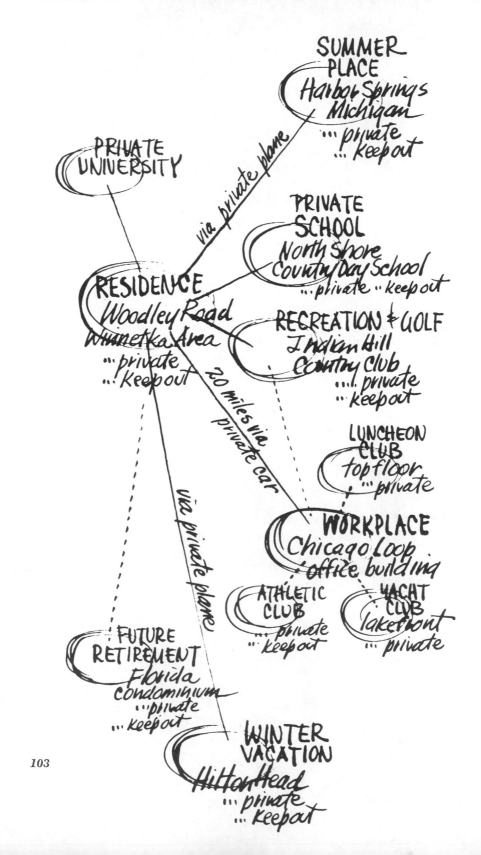

104. *Beating around the bush in Anchorage, Alaska, means flying. Plane ownership is so common that planes are sold on the main street. The city claims the largest plane ownership per capita in the United States.*

105. *Line-up for afternoon passengers: at northwest corner of Hemming Park in downtown Jacksonville, Florida, taxicabs and local residents, mostly black, rendezvous for a quick run north.*

to even out their coverage; they plot the known beats of criminals. I mapped my own daily beats for several weeks while writing this book, and was surprised at the frequency of one funny looking loop representing trips from a semi-suburban magazine office to an old downtown. Once plotted on paper, beats take on another aspect, revealing waste ("Was that trip really necessary?"), opportunities, and unnoticed regularities.

New beats may appear suddenly as the result of shifts in costs, especially of transportation. For example, during afternoon rush hours in downtown Jacksonville, I have observed that every few seconds a black shopper or commuter strolls up to a line of taxicabs waiting at the northwest corner of Hemming Park, headed north on North Hogan Street. He or she stoops down, asks where the cab is going, and eventually gets in. When the cab is filled, it usually heads northeast where a large proportion of Jacksonville's blacks live (fig. 105). This became a new beat as the result of zone fares set up on June 10, 1971, whereby passengers could be taken from Hemming Park to their door for as little as thirty-five cents if they lived in one of two close-in zones. On the bus, however, you pay thirty cents, follow the bus's regular beat, and there is a longer wait. As I watched at Hemming Park, six cabs filled and took off in about five minutes.

The Buildup of the Beat

Gradually we are organizing an increasing percentage of our daily movements into beats. What may seem like an impromptu "run down to the beach" or a "dash over to the shopping center" is part of an accumulating buildup of beats. This is another aspect of population increase, of heavier traffic, of the need to make every trip pay and, thus, plan our movements. A decade ago Jane Jacobs described, in *The Death and Life of Great American Cities,* the "intricate sidewalk ballet" that took place around 8 A.M. in front of her West Greenwich Village home in New York.[4] Hers was also a description of dozens of morning beats interlocking: garbagemen collecting, school kids walking, laundrymen delivering, shopkeepers opening, taximen cruising, and Mrs. Robert Jacobs putting out her family's garbage can before becoming a short-range commuter to an uptown job.

Describing Philadelphia's beats when he was that city's planning director, Edmund N. Bacon has observed that the city is composed of "a simultaneous movement system."[5] It may help to picture all traffic jams as tangles at the confluence of many beats. And as we look at such movements today, we observe that random movement, the free play of

106. *Keeping track of build-up of Chicago's traffic beats, reporter for Chicago radio shortwaves his sightings to station for broadcast. Position on top of John Hancock Building, 100 stories up, enables him to compete with helicopters.*

107. *When schedules tighten, traffic grows unpredictable and routes uncertain, more and more of the beat-bound public turns to outside advisors—auto clubs, helicopter traffic patrols, friends, and tipsters. Typical problem area, 1972, is Philadelphia. AAA map shows strangers how to navigate local traffic currents.*

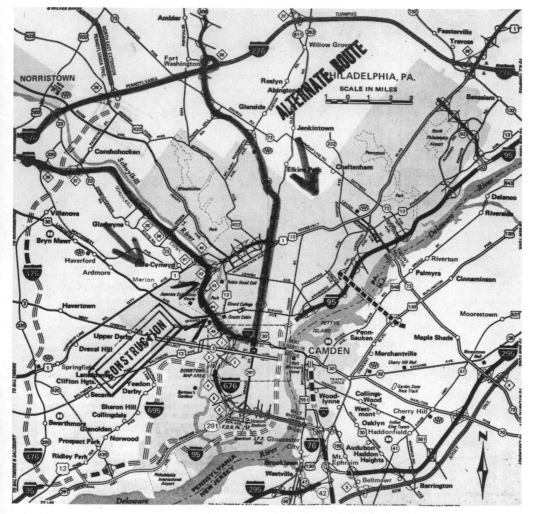

the mobile human being afoot, ahorseback, or in vehicles, is slowly rigidifying and being scheduled into beats (fig. 106).

This means that before making a move, each of us must make complex computations, often unconsciously: musing in the doorway before leaving for work, checking a shopping list before switching on the car's ignition key, or stopping at the station for gas *and* a map. Ours has become a check-listed, calendared, scheduled society. Beat planning has become so complex that my local AAA reports a five-year increase of 20 per cent in the number of Trip-tiks issued to its members (fig. 107). Trip-tiks are thicker today than a few years back: they have twenty-six preprinted pages of hints and instructions inserted ahead of the page that actually maps your route. There is also an 8-inch square emergency red sign, "SEND HELP," in case you get in a wreck. "Turn to us before you get in a jam," advertises a Jacksonville radio station. "For a short stay you will need a fast tan," urges the Sea & Ski suntan lotion pitch from a Florida billboard.

So beats require tuning in, mapping, musing, checking, pondering, planning—and no breakdowns. Nobody can stick to the beat when the

108

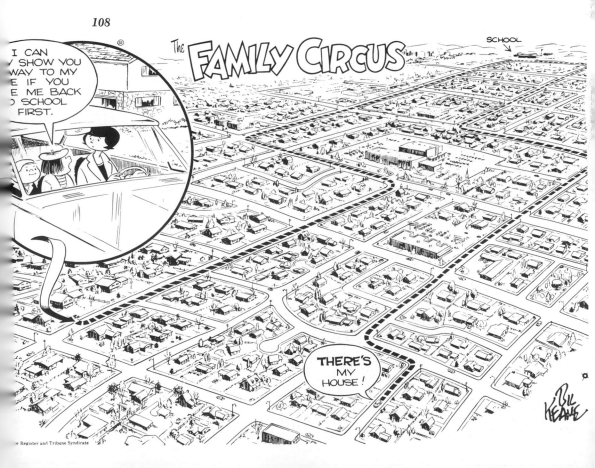

car battery dies or the subway conks out. So we spend more time and money fixing and replacing machines to keep us on the beat.

Mothers once did their own mental computer runs to figure out safe routes between home and school for their kids, but this beat is increasingly calculated and mapped by school officials (fig. 108). Such is the invisible reality behind the presence of guards at school intersections. Another form of reality: the sight of elderly and often white-haired men serving as school crossing guards in the Newport Pier section of Balboa Beach, California. They are clues to the nature of the town's population, which includes many retirees having little to do during what they consider a cold winter. Do not all societies put their population surpluses to work at such marginal jobs?

The Big Beat Changes

In and out, inhale-exhale, compression-expansion: for the first century of their growth most American cities could be depended upon to send out this single, overwhelming rhythmic message from their working beats. Many generations have learned to tell the time of day by the rattle of commuter trains, the noise of rush hour traffic that heads toward mid-city in the mornings and outward at night.

But the traffic streams no longer all point downtown, but rather in every direction, and one encounters queueing, stacking, tightening, and galloping—those phenomena of rush-hour traffic—far out on the urban fronts and no longer exclusively on the old radial, spoke-of-the-wheel routes. "Trips related to the old center city now comprise only a small part of daily travel in metropolitan areas," reported the President's Task Force on Suburban Problems in 1968.[6]

To drive through the open rolling countryside of the newtown of Irvine, California, near Newport Beach, at 7:45 A.M. and suddenly be caught in half-mile-long lines of commuters waiting to get through the traffic-lighted intersection of Jamboree Road and MacArthur Boulevard is a puzzling experience. But lift your gaze to the horizon; then you realize that those distant shoeboxes are commuter destinations—dynamic clusters of aero-based company offices, the International Chemical and Nuclear Corporation Research Center, and warehouses serving the nearby Orange County Airport and this boom-town region (fig. 109). Hence the open-country jams.

To get caught in bumper-to-bumper traffic through Tobesofkee Swamp on Highway 247 south of Macon, Georgia, in late afternoon makes no sense at all—until we recognize that Warner Robins Air Force Base, built at frantic speed in World War II and still a big job center in open coun-

109. A horizon of commuter destinations in newtown of Irvine, California, under development on giant Irvine Ranch south of Los Angeles.

try, has just released part of its load into the twenty-four-hour flow of some 34,000 vehicles between the base and Macon.

All beats set up counterpart movements. Daily at 7 A.M., for example, the beat begins at Kenilworth, Illinois, an upper-income suburb north of Chicago, as executives and professionals head for work. A journalist observer from Northwestern University reported, "On the heels of the resident exodus . . . the workers move in. Postmen, leaf rakers, delivery-men, handymen, and maids converge upon the area."[7] At certain morning hours, key intersections which link service and industrial areas to middle- to upper-income residential districts become crammed with delivery vans of every sort. At such a junction I recently found myself in a line with eight service vans, including a platoon of white, yellow, and blue tele-phone repair trucks on their daily beats from service center to house calls. Platoons do not happen; they are ordered and dispatched. As parts of larger systems, they are valuable clues to the way systems interact.

Beats Within Beats

Beats tend to generate their own language. A taxi driver in Eugene, Oregon, described a local hotel run to me as "a ten-minute hustle to the airport." More often the phrase is "a $3.50 run from downtown," and in Detroit it runs up to $12.

A patrolman responds to his orders by following the beat assigned to him, mapped from a sergeant's memory of his days on the beat, plus what the computer or the grapevine says is happening out there. A patrolman or a news reporter is considered fit for his beat when he begins to know what to expect from his environment and can handle it. Each has achieved a fit with environment after first having sized it up by measuring its demands against his own time and energy resources.

Beat mastery may be found in all walks of life. Dean William L. C. Wheaton of the College of Environmental Design, University of California, observed during a Times Square inspection in Manhattan that "the hustlers walk against the traffic so they can avoid the fuzz [police] and display the goods."[8] In some of Florida's larger cities, "the streetwalkers don't walk, they cover their beats in Cadillacs," observed June

110. Once a busy port of call for impatient miners and railroadmen patronizing a then-flourishing whore-house district east of the Wabash River, now the neighborhood is mostly cleared, inactive, and these cottages behind solid walls are only remnants of a once busy scene at Terre Haute, Indiana.

111. *"World's Largest Classic Car Show"—the 17th annual Auburn-Cord-Duesenberg Festival has transformed Auburn, Indiana, by putting it on the Labor Day weekend beat of some 30,000 classic-car fans.*

Cleo and Hank Mesouf in their *Florida: Polluted Paradise*.[9] On one-way Commercial Street in Provincetown, Massachusetts, I have observed during the height of the August tourist season that homosexual queens appear to work the east side of the street, which is closer to the main, Highway 6 approach routes for newcomers. A similar position athwart the crucial movement system of prospective customers was occupied by a formerly flourishing whore-house district in Terre Haute, Indiana, now reduced to a historic remnant (fig. 110).

Seasonal and Annual Beats

"There's no place on earth that does not have at least a 25 per cent seasonal pulse," observes ecologist Howard T. Odum,[10] and most travelers in the 1970's would raise him at least 50 per cent, especially in July and August. To travel during tourist season is to encounter that crowd phcnomenon known locally as Frontier Day (Cheyenne, Wyoming, and points west); The Great Shrimp Boat Race (Fernandina Beach, Florida); Cheese Day (Logan, Utah); Bonneville (Utah) National Speed Trials, also called Amateur Week on the Salt Flats; Derby Week (Louisville, Kentucky); Race Week (Indianapolis, Indiana); Clam Festival (Pismo Beach, California); the International Azalea Festival (Norfolk, Virginia); or, simply, Court Day, the County Fair, the Great Homecoming Day—any of which has become a festival. (See fig. 111.) During spring dogwood and fall leaf-turning seasons, sightseers turn U.S. Highway 25 through the Great Smoky Mountains into a fifty-mile traffic jam centered on the sights and resorts of Gatlinburg, Tennessee. Spring vacation raises the pulse rate at a thousand beach resorts, and "when ski lodges have carnivals at the same time, the road from Salt Lake City to Snowbird gets completely blocked, "commented Jerry McCoy of the University of Utah.[11] When deer season opens, the streets of Santa Fe, New Mexico, are jammed with hunters' jeeps. At every hand, art fairs are blocking more miles of streets every year as neighborhoods gain new influence over their own turf.

Now that important national holidays have been jiggered around on the calendar, we now celebrate George Washington's birthday, Memorial Day, Columbus Day, Veterans Day, among others, invariably on Mondays. This shift from midweek now makes it possible to pack vacation trips into longer weekends, so that highways leading back home to Appalachia from Detroit, Dayton, Cincinnati, and other centers are more than ever jampacked around major holidays.

Consequently, travel offers a grab bag of unpredictable encounters. Nobody is mapping these huge beats and jams. All travel is a risk unless the traveler wants to forget schedules, get off the road, lock the car, merge with the crowd in some unsuspected celebration, drink and dance in the courthouse square to celebrate some great event hitherto unknown except to local celebrants. Thus travel tips must be traded among friends. At Gainesville, I have heard University of Florida faculty members argue over whether it is easier to drive from their mid-state campus to Anastasia Island, Flagler Beach, or Crescent Beach some seventy-five miles east on the Atlantic coast, than to go westward to Cedar Key about ninety minutes away on the Gulf coast, debating the relative weekend rigors of each route.

There is a Friday afternoon buildup in Chicago's traffic beginning every April; it gets progressively tighter every week, especially on sunny days. The reason is simple: more and more mass-transit commuters begin driving their cars to work on Friday mornings, hoping to beat the rush hour in getting away for weekends and/or do some pre-weekend shopping. The elevators in New York City's CBS Building become crowded in late fall, beginning early on Friday mornings, as skiers show up equipped for the weekend, skis and all, thus reducing the capacity of each elevator below its specified load.[12]

The reason drivers on interstate routes suddenly come upon those great highway "Food–Gas" strings and clusters of motels and gas stations is that they are all ganged up to capture travelers at the end of a particular beat, at predictable intervals. Most tourists' beats shape up into four-hour increments, or modules, of human behavior, according to Professor Richard Wilkinson of North Carolina State University. He observes that "the entire trip is structured about these units" and that "whole areas or districts [of new resorts] can logically be structured with these increments in mind."[13]

Take that sign outside the airport at Portland, Oregon, which says "Come home this summer—Continental to Denver [fig. 112]." Fly home? Who flies home? Asking these questions, I found Portland to be a city loaded with people from someplace else, especially the West and Midwest. What is more natural, if they have the price, than to fly east for holidays and reunions? A shuttle parking-lot operator outside the airport told me his 150-car lot is jammed every Christmas by Portlanders "going home."[14] So that sign unlocks the eastward back-home beats of thousands of Pacific Northwest families.

But movement has its costs. When beats converge during rush hours in Los Angeles, susceptible people on certain freeways begin to suffer from carbon monoxide and other pollutants. Eventually such cities will be

112

metering, managing, and regulating the traffic's beat so as to overload neither freeways nor the air above them. Experiments are under way, from London to Los Angeles, in electronically administering the traffic beat, just as electronic regulators are being installed in patients with irregular heartbeats to get them back on the beat.

Places of First Resort

At the end of many beats lie resorts, spas, vacation spots, and special-purpose retreats whose manufacture and operation is one of the nation's fastest-growing industries.

Resorts do not look like other places, as the Texas travel and "vacationscape" specialist Clare Gunn has noted: "The shift from accepting tourists as guests to catering to them as consumers has changed the entire face of the land."[15] The resort landscape has a distinctive look; it is full of special objects: portable, collapsible, transportable, movable, expandable. They serve as shelters, furniture, windbreaks, partitions, storage, and transport. They may be boats turned upside down in winter to shelter lawn furniture, lawnmowers, etc.; trailers up on blocks packed with summer camping stuff or stacked with tourist tackle; anachronistic lobster pots, rental surfboards, cartoned suntan lotion. One views the off-season resort as a scene of make-ready.

As for resorters, once removed from their old self-serving scenes back home, they preen themselves into special uniforms and costumes which later may get translated into year-round gear. Thus resorts may be viewed as special hunting grounds for life-style pushers and fashion hustlers. To succeed at this game, resorts must provide fitting rooms for trying on a new self, so it is no wonder that the resort landscape resembles a high-fashion stage set for home movies: golf courses crammed with photogenic props, beaches with photogenic guards, waterfront dominated by clues such as non-navigational lighthouses—backgrounds for such rituals as family snapshots, weddings, or picnics. Thus millions of vacationers pursue avidly the vacation beats, eager to be separated from their old selves in special-purpose settings (fig. 113).

Avoidance Areas of Last Resort

For every traffic jam there is a gap, for every beat there is a void—a place of last resort, one that has been drained of activity, spooked, abandoned for the nonce. Places such as the low-activity zone of empty auto-sales lots south of Houston's business center; and parts of the ill-fated Pruitt-Igoe public housing in St. Louis, half-empty, partly burned out, and

113. *No resort or historic mecca is complete without its tourist tackle, such as Williamsburg, Virginia's stocks in which visitors may go through "photogenic" routines to prove they have been there—i.e., to the Public Gaol.*

tenanted by the poorest disadvantaged blacks, before vast sums were spent to demolish some of the buildings and rebuild others into a more humane community. Especially in the early 1970's there began to emerge whole neighborhoods of empty tenement and apartment districts in New York City and elsewhere, victimized by speculators, abandoned by tenants, plundered by passersby.

Unless they become fire hazards or threaten the larger community, most unofficial avoidance areas are well-kept secrets.* Newspapers sel-

* One such map of "anxiety areas" in downtown Detroit was prepared by the staff of the City Plan Commission based on a small cross section of interviews with downtown office workers. After the above comments were written, permission to publish that map in this book was denied by the Commission director.

dom identify them on maps until conditions get officially labeled, for fear of protest from outraged property owners. Boosterism, fear, and pride conspire to shield them from public scrutiny, especially in the early stages. A stranger may observe boarded-up buildings, gang slogans spray-painted on walls, may get hard-look signals and hard talk from the residents. But for the most part, the designation of avoidance areas is informal, which means: look hard, ask around first, and do not barge in.

LOOMING QUIETLY as a backdrop in thousands of neighborhoods is a huge, piled-up mass of something-or-other. It just sits there quietly. Nobody pays it heed. Bulldozers snort around and nibble at its hindquarters. Trucks come and go, raising dust, paying tribute, leaving deposits, scurrying away.

And then one day it starts to burn, and, if the thing is made of sawdust or sulphur, the air turns nasty and the neighborhood flees; or if it is made of waste sludge or culm it may simply shift from inertia to movement, slipping and sliding and smothering all in the vicinity (fig. 114); or if it is building stone and nobody is using stone any longer, the pile may sit unmolested for years, the lumpy proletariat of the landscape.

Such a scenario gets played out wherever manufacturers depend on raw materials concentrated into local heaps, piles, tanks, or—the term I prefer—"stacks." Nobody puts stacks on tourists' maps, and everybody conspires to act as though they were not there. For raw materials are considered low-class stuff, economically and socially; they have been piled up on the wrong side of the tracks and worked over by low-wage labor. Consequently a neighborhood dominated by stacks has its own high density of clues even though it may be shoved into a backwater as the city's least visible of all districts.

I am using stack to mean a high-density mass of materials, minerals, objects, liquids, or energy, concentrated by man's efforts, which exerts

Stacks

significant impact upon its environment as it shifts to a horizontal distribution pattern.

Stacks remind us—orange sawdust piles, slag foothills, brown pine-stump humps, yellow sulphur mountains, calcium chloride moraines, pulpwood log sierras, and fuel tank farms—that the business of cutting, crushing, refining, pumping, hauling, and handling basic materials holds the key to understanding the workings of hundreds of urban places (figs. 115 and 116). North of Highway 66 along Foothill Drive through Claremont, California, one still sees huge piles of white glacial boulders extending for blocks through old orange groves and new subdivisions. They were painstakingly hand-piled by Cahuilla Indians and Chinese

114. Covering hundreds of acres, this stack of waste carbide slurry from synthetic rubber production at Rubbertown, southeast of Louisville, Kentucky, collapsed—covering buildings, cars, roads. Some twenty years in the making, it had prospect in 1972 of finding an economic re-use.

115. Port Wentworth on Savannah River: plant of Continental Can Company Paperboard and Kraft Paper Division. Pine-stump piles protected from prowlers by fence and guardhouse. Photographer refused entry, May 23, 1971.

116. Highly visible clues to one of the basic economic forces in the Vancouver, British Columbia, economy—those giant floating log rafts in nearby rivers.

laborers before World War I to clear land for orange groves, and remain today almost immovable.[1] Only that highly energetic process of subdividing the land for expensive lots is likely to displace them.

Potential for change is the key; all stacks are, or were, part of a process that offers clues to the presence or absence of those basic urban goings on, manufacturing, storing, or warehousing. They indicate surpluses of goods, all of which mean potential energy that can lead to local specialization of jobs and differentiation of human activities.

Examine closely these big stack operations. You will observe that they often dominate their surroundings visually, even though they may remain physically and politically apart. To the uninitiated, many such stacks suddenly loom up in city or countryside with no warning beyond the ever-present high fence and "Keep Out" sign.

"But why here?" you ask. The answer may lie in local sources of cheap raw materials, or in cheap labor, or in feeble anti-pollution regulations, or in subsidies both hidden and open, inducing the stack operators to stay and provide jobs in backward or underdeveloped regions. Such a form of stack shelter may be seen at Fernandina Beach, Florida, where the giant Container Corporation of America, and ITT-Rayonier paper plants[2] enjoy the legal privilege of using the Amelia River and Atlantic Ocean as sinks into which they dump millions of gallons of wastes daily, producing a foamy wake a mile long behind cruisers on the river and brownish foam on the beach surf.

Locations offer many clues: the oldest stacks often mark the edges of the nineteenth-century city although many survive only on historical markers showing where old tanneries, grist and woolen mills, brickyards, gas works, and railroads once lined the millrace that brought power and the creeks which carried away sewage. In New England, the nineteenth-century textile mills, docks, and sheds are mostly gone, but the old workers' tenements straggling up the hills and down the valleys still survive as evidence.

Thus along the Willamette River in Portland, Oregon, owners of rotting, nineteenth-century lumber docks and warehouses on MacAdam Avenue were busy making plans in the 1970's for the next generation of users—fancy marinas and high-cost condominium apartments to replace the old stacktown. Lumber stacks are moving out to be replaced by more profitable, mechanized operators. Thirty-one forest-product plants and sawmills were operating in the 1920's on the banks of Portland's rivers; by 1971 there remained only six.[3]

Finally, you observe that since the 1950's the big stacks have shifted outward, sometimes ten to thirty miles from the old city. As Constantinos Doxiadis once commented, "Foreign elements have always found places to alight outside the city gates."[4] As large-scale processing of raw materials requires more space for employee parking, containerized stacking, room for future expansion and for parasitic, subsidiary, or supplier firms to move next door, they move farther outward and extend the workings of the daily urban system another mile or two.

If the people of "stacktown" do no more than dig in the mines, cut trees, and pile up materials to be processed elsewhere, they are likely to remain, like the banana plantation workers of the Dominican Republic, the nickel miners at Thompson, Manitoba, or the pulpwood mill workers of St. Mary's, Georgia, stuck in the nineteenth-century mode with twentieth-century machines, dependent upon one employer and upon fluctuations in the world price of one basic material or crop.

Furthermore, stacktown tends to use local land, water, air, and people as parts of its disposal system, and gets away with it. It distributes noise for neighbors to absorb in the vicinity of dynamite-using quarries; spews effluvia and dust for local residents to breathe (as along Brighton Boulevard, north of Denver); spreads chemical smells through parts of Buffalo, New York; pours sulfurous fumes from paper mills to be air-drifted over scores of southern cities; billows clouds from such edge-of-the-city locations as the Anaconda copper mills southwest of Salt Lake City; piles its

117. When an inadequate dam of mine waste ruptured on February 26, 1972, it let loose a wall of black water that killed at least 118 persons, destroyed almost 1,000 dwellings, and did some $20 million damage along Buffalo Creek valley in southern West Virginia.

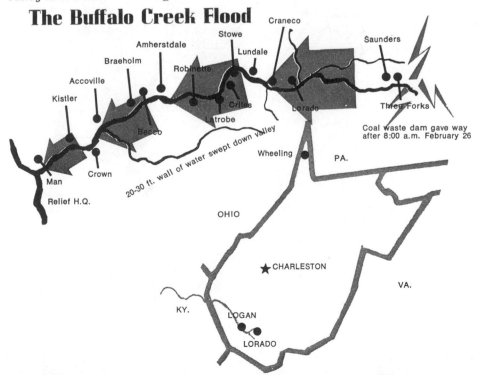

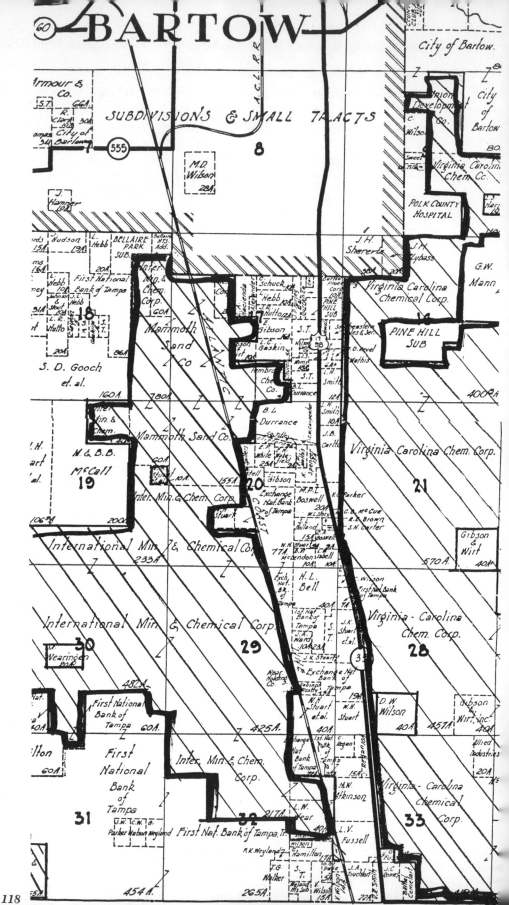

mining wastes in narrow valleys forming dams that may, and sometimes do, rupture and destroy everything downstream (fig. 117); spills oil with impunity and ubiquity onto closed waters and open land. After eye-and-nose tests in scores of cities, I have been forced to conclude: if it is a raw-materials stacktown, it stinks—and vice versa.

To well-informed eyes and noses, stacktown is still in the early industrial revolution, with raw power and raw materials just next door, stacked in the open. Stacktown's end products are often far down in the chain of complexity; it makes money from a single stage of production—handling basic foods, converting raw materials into first-stage products, grinding local trees into pulp and brown paper, pulverizing phosphate rock into fertilizer, ripsawing logs into dimension lumber, mining and shipping coal, pumping and refining oil. The big ones are big: U.S. Steel added over $1.2 billion worth of improvements to its Gary, Indiana, plant in ten years.[5] They take up lots of space: Union Camp Corporation's plant occupies the 450-acre site of the old Hermitage Plantation near Savannah, Georgia, and manages over one million acres of pineland to supply its mill.[6]

Behind the older stacks is a town often stuck in old power relationships: unsophisticated jobs are controlled by a few big firms (fig. 118); this is a no-nonsense, no-Ph.D. town, the fief of old monopolies and/or new conglomerates. Its blue-collar citizens tend to vote against bond issues for civic centers, opera houses, and institutions of higher education which come to be seen in stacktown as pet activities of the rich local elite.

Stacktowns tend to be absentee owned, which also describes so much of the nation's basic resources: timber stacks in the Pacific Northwest, New England mountains, and along the 900-mile pine-plantation belt from the Carolinas to Texas. The great petro-chemical, paperboard, acoustic tile, plastics, and fiberboard plants for the most part have gone national. If the signs on the chain link fences out front do not, the public relations man in the office will—refer inquiries to the head office far away.

Stacking in the Streets

Many businesses start outdoors—in the backyard (fig. 119), on the street or sidewalk; many survive by pre-empting public space for storage, processing their goods, negotiation, coffee breaks, and use as conveyor belts. New York's Seventh Avenue garment district would fold up tomorrow were it not permitted to use the streets as conveyor belts—where

18. *Outsiders' ownership of the great phosphate beds underlying much of Polk County, Florida, are reflected in corporate names of mining companies on this city map.*

scurrying porters tie up traffic as they push rolling racks of dresses from shop to distributor (fig. 120).

In stacktown, a visitor finds it difficult to tell what is public and what is private (fig. 121). That loading dock there—is it public or is it an extension of a private building into public space? Go east a few blocks from Manhattan's World Trade Center to Greene Street and see how the sidewalks were converted into semicontinuous truck-loading platforms, or

119. Segregationist attitudes toward raw materials, second-hand equipment, etc., tend to push such old stuff into the background, but many family incomes depend on back and front yards stacked with trading goods, such as around this hillside house in North Carolina.

120. *Pre-emption of public streets by long occupancy in the garment district of New York City. Streets are essential part of the low-cost production lines extending from nearby textile company buildings, sometimes directly into sales-rooms of Manhattan stores.*

121. *Clueful scene west of downtown Baltimore: all day parking for 75 cents, indicating low land rents; sidewalk is taken over for wastepaper business, which generally means that few other claims are being put on the same space.*

watch the transition in old warehouse districts such as in St. Louis (fig. 122).

The process of stacking and loading heavy raw materials and goods carves out many such indelible shapes within the city. Go take a look at the Blitz-Weinhard Company (beer) stockhouses, on the northeast corner of Twelfth and Couch streets, Portland, Oregon. What might have been a sidewalk along Couch Street has been converted into an elevated loading platform between warehouse and freight cars standing on rails within the street. To a stranger, streets in this vicinity appear little more than railroad tracks whose chief function is to provide access to warehouse docks and floors. Blitz-Weinhard shows how stacking can remain a semi-downtown activity, moving its heavy stuff indoors while leaving streets open for some auto and truck movement.

122. Way back when railroad tracks, loading docks, and heavy freight were all concentrated downtown, the neighborhood was designed for a single purpose—with rails and docks instead of pedestrian sidewalks. These remain. So will this St. Louis, Missouri, warehouse. New owner (Washington University, 1972) pays no property taxes, hence can rent the building competitively. A tax-paying owner might well have torn it down.

The presence of large and active stacks and stacking operations in mid-city is a quick clue to local power and who holds it, especially in smaller towns such as Jellico, Tennessee (1960 population: 1,800). The continued (1972) presence of freight cars loading pulpwood directly across the street from the biggest variety store in town—fork-lift trucks on one side, baby buggies on the other—is a clue to the long-time power of a railroad in such a raw-materials town (fig. 123). Above all, stacktown is a scene in transition, as changes in technology wreak profound dislocations upon the local landscape, especially in regions with little power to make their own decisions.

"As industries age, they rationalize, mechanize, and seek cheaper labor," observes economist Wilbur R. Thompson. "This is the old Southern lament . . . the industries slide down the learning curve. The towns like Greenville, S.C., have to get more industries just to stand still. You stand

123. Stacktown scene in Jellico, Tennessee, still predominantly a raw-materials town where pulpwood is loaded on freight cars smack in the middle of town. Big change in the early 1970's—old tracks were ripped up, to be replaced by parking lot (beyond stacks).

there in North Carolina and watch the textile plants come through from New England en route to the Philippines."[7]

Thus, in order to absorb the most clues from stacktown, one must follow the process, noting who controls it and how it is being altered. A "hardening" of goods in storage, for example: do you observe at your neighborhood lumber yard that rough-sawed lumber is no longer stacked, and that the stock is all semifinished? Or, do you notice that red, clay tile pipe has disappeared from the plumber's supply yard and that only metal pipe is now in stock (fig. 124)? These shifts may indicate that the profit margin has dropped on rough or lightweight products, that taxes have gone up forcing a change to higher-margin items, that the business has changed hands, or that the owners are packing in the higher-profit items before selling out. Something is going on. One such clue can suggest many directions in which to look next.

124. What passers-by see on this wholesaler's lot is steel pipe instead of the bright red, clay tile sewer pipe stored there until 1972. Breakage of clay pipe outran the wholesaler's profit, and cost of hand-caulking joints made it unpopular with contractors. So dealer switched from clay to metal. East Market Street, Louisville, Kentucky.

125. *A highly specialized landscape, at first glance rather barren and mundane. This is a dangerous-movement zone outside a giant limestone quarry (entrance, left) near the confluence of the Ohio, Tennessee, and Cumberland rivers. Everybody across the road stands well back to avoid gravel trucks. Whatever once stood on the concrete pedestal (left) has long ago been abandoned.*

DMZs

On highways outside many a mineral stacktown, the clues multiply and the ground shakes as giant trucks come barreling down from the mines or quarries. I have watched them in Kentucky and West Virginia while the world price for coal caused local booms in auger and deep-slope mining in the early 1970's. The roads are potholed, the dust is black, and everybody stands back when coal moves downhill.

Or, stand in the streets of college-and-lumber town, Eugene, Oregon, a few hundred yards north of the Civic Center, and watch the giant loggers' rigs swerve through the intersection. Fresh snow from logging sites in the mountains spills onto the streets, and God help the driver or anyone in the way if that load shifts or gets loose on that long, winding trail down from the hills far away to the lumber mill dock in the valley.

Such places are the dangerous movement zones or DMZ's in regions which produce a preponderance of heavy materials from mines, farms, forests, pits, quarries, and fields. These are special, clue-laden, recognizable places (fig. 125). Everybody in the vicinity knows them and ac-

126. When a paving contractor's own mailbox gets knocked over and stays upended, this tells even the most casual passer-by that he is running through a DMZ, even though the neighborhood (eastern Indianapolis suburbs) is mostly residential.

127. Streets around major Detroit auto manufacturing plants become part of the production line as trucks (here hauling engines down main drag of Hamtramck) occasionally dominate lesser traffic.

cepts their risks as part of everyday life. The DMZ's seldom appear on any map or AAA Trip-tik. Even local traffic accident maps may not emphasize the hazards (fig. 126).

DMZ highways become the turf of the heavy haulers, which literally convert roads, highways, and streets into extensions of the production line of nearby mines, fields, mills, and factories. The highways become part of local contractors' production systems, hauling prefabricated hous-

Staff Photo by Frank Ashley

HEAVY COAL TRUCKS are again using KY 15 near Vicco, even though a resurfacing project on a six-mile stretch of the road between Hazard and Whitesburg has not been completed.

Coal firms won't be asked to pay for wrecked road

By FRANK ASHLEY
Courier-Journal Staff Writer

HAZARD, Ky.—A plan well-publicized during the administration of former Gov. Louie B. Nunn to force area coal operators to pay for repairs to a rutted, crumbling section of new highway near here apparently will not be pushed by the administration of Gov. Wendell H. Ford.

The 2-year-old six-mile stretch of KY

ministration, reaffirmed the department's commitment, made in December 1970, to collect the "whole amount or a portion of damages" from the operators. A month later he reported the department was gathering information for a possible court fight to force the industry to pay.

Now, almost a year and a half after the plan was announced, the Ford administra-

ing components and earth fill from one point to another. They overload the public roads, flout the speed limits, and exert powerful political influence against tougher regulations and enforcements (figs. 127, 128, and 129).

At its worst, stacktown is a primitive form of human settlement, preoccupied with rooting profits from its environment and with putting little back. It may become more complex and civilized later, but one should not be surprised that stacktown voters burn in effigy (if not in fact) a conservationist who proposes to shut down the local paper mill for polluting the river. For those seeking to change stacktown's mode of operation, the road is a rocky one. Unless one is willing to stick in there for a long, and ultimately political, fight, one is advised: do not look, do not sniff, stand back—or leave town.

129. To avoid becoming a DMZ, this community sets its own rules as to who can do what on the road. Vicinity of Corvallis, Oregon.

Sɪɴᴋs ᴀʀᴇ places of last resort into which powerful groups in society shunt, shove, dump, and pour whatever or whomever they do not like or cannot use: auto carcasses, garbage, trash, and minority groups. American society acts as though all these were identical undesirable elements to be pushed over the bank, heaved off the edge, out of sight, out of mind, down into the sink.

Sinks are special-purpose places produced in such predictable quantities by American cities that it would appear that a form of geopolitical conspiracy has been at work. For all cities create sinks. Some regions are turned into sinks for other regions or for the nation and must abjectly seek or accept wastes, industries, and activities no other place wants.

Sinks have one timeless aspect—a topographical awkwardness which makes them uninhabitable or undesirable by current middle-class standards. Sinks are apt to be swampy, low-lying, or otherwise difficult to develop. Sinks are inaccessible, either by nature or by man's contrivance. Many sinks have a bad name going back to nineteenth-century typhoid or malaria epidemics.

Most North American sinks are unseen from the main drag or from the best addresses, shut off by maze-like streets or roundabout approaches, tucked or sequestered away from the view of the vocal upper and middle classes. Many sinks lie in the shadows of old industries, where they stay

130. *Now the site of Techwood Homes, first New Deal public housing project, Atlanta's Tanyard Creek had gone through usual industrialization-slum cycle as 1937 photo shows. Creek is now underground.*

drenched in the smell, or doused in the dust and swill, of their more powerful neighbors upstage and upwind.

So noxious were many historic sinks that they became prime targets for public-health reformers in the nineteenth century, public housers in the 1930's (fig. 130), and urban renewers and highway engineers in the 1950's and into the present. In the process, hundreds of sinks have been filled and their residents dispersed, their old springs and streams bull-dozed or piped underground with consequent loss of their scenic and biotic potential.

Sink Screening

We have taken sink-making as a natural process for so long that its products have become almost invisible. Consequently in looking at my own city I learned to force my eyes to obey the law of gravity, to pursue the slope, to follow the flows, to seek the sink.

Not surprisingly, it is in the South where sinks have been reinforced by generations of custom, that sink-making is so subtle, and topography is so often a clue to social geography. On the eastern shore of Maryland, atop gentle ridges and high ground sit the courthouses and big churches, the haunts of the whites; in the creek valleys and by the sloughs one is more likely to find the blacks. The profile of vertical segregation is occasionally crystal clear. In most American cities, the richer you are, the less likely you are to confront the sinks; the poorer you are, the harder it is to climb out.

Shouldered into hundreds of such places were freed slaves after the Civil War and European immigrants of the late nineteenth century. Similar pressures were put upon blacks who migrated to southern cities after the Civil War, and during the great waves of black migration into northern cities during and after World War I and II. No wonder the rise in black power in the 1960's and the demand for self-determination among black ghetto residents caught white America by surprise. The sink, where blacks generally lived, had been historically sequestered and hence was invisible. There was "no such place" in the eyes of the white establishment; and the techniques of ensuring that there was no such place were many and complex.

First off, there was the name changing. Black Mud Lane, in my own Louisville, was altered to Rangeland Road to get rid of old wet-woods connotations and to help sell new houses. Swampy Little Africa, long since drained, has now been upgraded to become Southwick. And all across the Piedmont Crescent cities of North Carolina, names long ago tacked onto slum valleys—Black Bottom, Haiti (locally "hay-tie"), and Monkey Bottom—have been wiped off the map and more genteel names substituted. One Billy Goat Hill I know has been given the whitewashed name of Angora Heights.

Consequent to such widespread name changing, today's tourist or other city-watcher must go to special lengths for clues to ferret out the sinks. Nor will he get much help from standard sources, most of which are notoriously unwilling to reveal the detailed nature and frequency of local hazards such as floods (fig. 131), landslides, earthquakes, hurricanes, tornadoes, or the exact nature of local sinks.

Of the half million newcomers to Phoenix and Maricopa County, Arizona, in recent years, few would suspect that the canyons, washes, and wadis forming a lacework through that seemingly flat landscape of the valleys are, in fact, sinks in disguise. Newcomers may occupy or even build in those gentle-looking swales, only to have the next rainstorm miles away deliver a gush of water down the wash, sweeping away all in its path. One needs a wary eye for all such sinks, since few promotional maps will reveal their presence (fig. 132).

Old local customs die hard, and in recent years it has been the federal highway program which—despite its many faults—has opened up many a local sink. Let us see an example in Macon, Georgia, which unlike more cosmopolitan Atlanta 100 miles to the north had many generations of old-South attitudes to reinforce its sink-making. The first is the Forrest Avenue–Williams School neighborhood, a mile northwest of downtown Macon in a valley formed by a branch of Vineville Brook. Most of the residents are blacks occupying a typical backwater: access from downtown was tortuous and difficult until Interstate Highway 75 (from the Straits of Mackinac to St. Petersburg, Florida) was built in the 1960's and Wal-

131. Between floods, a discreet conspiracy of silence descends over the scene of the last disaster, such as here along the Ohio River near West Point, Kentucky. The conspirators make light of flood damage, heroes of flood victims, and little of the possibility that "100-year-floods" seem to come more often these days. Photo, 1964.

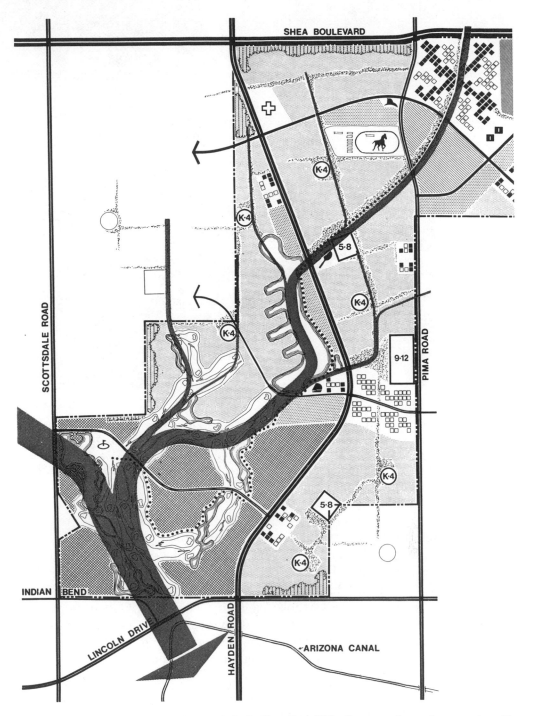

132. *How to rationalize a sink: Indian Bend Wash, a gentle swale occasionally carrying huge floodwaters, is to be widened, deepened, cleared of growth, realigned within western portion of the Kaiser-Aetna-McCormick Ranch in Scottsdale, Arizona. Plan shows how future floods are to be directed.*

133. Low-lying neighborhood in background occupied a break in street patterns along a creek and was sequestered for generations in Macon, Georgia, until Telfair Street (foreground) was cut through as a link to downtown First Street. Stone foundation wall (right) is evidence of earlier, higher Telfair Street level.

nut Street was extended into the sink through a small ridge that formed a topographic barrier west of historic College Street. Suddenly, this old black backwater has now become open, visible, and accessible. Exposure of another sink took place in the 1960's when Macon's First Street—the wide, brick-paved axis for City Hall, Chamber of Commerce, Civic Auditorium, and the 1828 First Presbyterian Church—was extended southward to join Telfair Street, thus connecting up another near-downtown sink around Carver and B. S. Ingram Schools (fig. 133).

Fragging

Thoughtlessly, all American cities continue manufacturing sinks through a process I will call "fragging." The meaning of the term got a new twist during the winding down of the Viet Nam War when dissident United States soldiers tried knocking out their own officers with fragmentation grenades. But long before this special meaning entered the scene, land developers and others were fragging the landscape with fragmentation tactics that left the landscape pockmarked with pieces of real estate, space, land, or topography ill-fitted for future human uses.

Your bedroom has been fragged if the builder left such a small space for the beds that you can hardly squeeze in a table or yourself. Your downtown has been fragged if the fraggers leave useless slots of spaces between buildings, between parking lots and fences, so as inevitably to invite trash dumpers (figs. 134, 135, and 136). Your highways are fragged by highway departments that straighten kinks and re-align roads but leave behind odd-shaped parcels of the sort one sees along highway Strips II to IV (see Chapter V). Thousands of neighborhoods are crammed with useless back lots, inaccessible tracts, alley lots with no alleys, non-negotiable rights-of-way, the millions of geographic errors which lash together every urbanized landscape, the product of slipshod platting and jackleg surveyors.

To be sure, thousands of such acres can be reassembled and replatted at exorbitant cost for some future renewal program when the demand warrants. But they stand idle today as evidence of the careless handling of landscape in the past.

134. Mini-sink on University Avenue, Gainesville, Florida: one of those fragments of building space exposed to every passing trash-tosser and vandal. A miniature version of what sometimes happens to neighborhoods and even whole regions.

135. *Fragments, slivers, leftovers, and oddments of city space immediately are turned into wastebaskets by the public, which correctly assumes that nobody gives a damn about such places so why not trash them up. Location: across street from downtown Stouffer's Inn, Cincinnati. Billboard shows "View of Tomorrow" map.*

136. *Even chain-link fence (left) doesn't protect this fragment of urban space between parking lot and building from usual trash-dumping by passers-by. On Sundays in Manhattan, New York, parking lot (background) is a busy, colorful Flea Market, 25th Street at Sixth Avenue.*

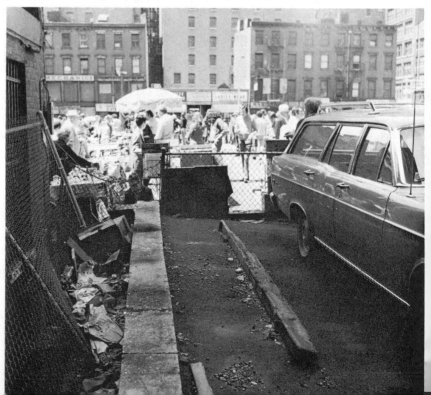

The Great Breath

Out of many another urban front, where most of the next 100 million Americans will find living space, prospective sinks wait their turns to be despoiled and sunk in the traditional manner.

But is it not clear that the traditional manner itself must be junked? Those swamps, sloughs, swales, cliffs, buttes, wadis, canyons, and difficult slopes are precisely the places that ought to be saved—as high-energy, ecologically productive reserves and as recreation areas for the community's health and benefit.

To see things this way means we have to reorder our vision as well as our priorities, and learn to view sinks with ecological insight. The moment we cross this visual threshold, we can look on a tidal marsh not as an inert site submissively awaiting the high-rise developer, but as the most productive, natural energy-transfer system in a coastal metropolitan area; i.e., not a vapid scene but a valued process. A salt marsh of Spartina grass is busy producing 3,500 grams of biomass per square meter per year —waterborne food materials as well as shrimp, oyster, crab, and fish— compared with 350 grams production from the best wheat land, 400 grams from corn, and 1,700 grams from sugarcane.

Pre-vision of this sort stresses process and continuity—and not the merely present objects of a man-made world. It enables us to see a sunrise, in the ecologist Howard T. Odum's words, as letting loose "a great breath as tons upon tons of oxygen are released [by sunlight] from the living photochemical surfaces of green plants which are becoming charged with food storages."[1] It reveals to us the torrents of oxygen pouring from a hillside forest, the gush of rainfall being sucked through forest duff and

137. *One way to reduce the conversion of waterways and valleys to sinks: all land not in development modules to be held as ecological reservoirs in public trust.*

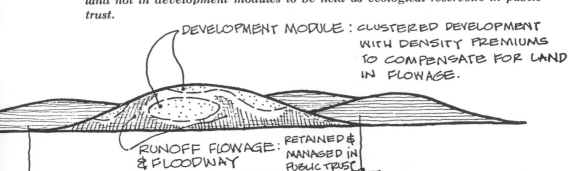

detritus and absorbed by root hairs; it shows us the two million forms of microbiotic life in every cubic centimeter of rich forest soil, and reveals to us the nightly run of owl, bat, skunk, possum, coon, etc., from the forest haunts into the surrounding neighborhood to tap their supply of mice, rats, grubs, and insects—and occasionally to raid gardens.

Pursuing these images further, we see the hills around San Francisco, California, being stripped and padded with rows of new houses, each destined to let loose predictable volumes of commuters onto the bay bridges into San Francisco, and each to spin off demands for new schools, churches, shopping centers, and for lawyers to fight zoning battles. We see the inexorable hard-surfacing of those new suburbs as cutting down the region's capacity to absorb storm waters, as another twelve inches added to the next flash flood from local streams, as another six inches of topsoil washed away in a generation, and as a future demand for expensive and ugly ditching of the region's natural streams.

Once we penetrate such a scene, once we calculate its alternate futures, we can then grasp the benefits which these hard-working elements can contribute to the urbanizing scene. Streams, swamps, and flowage zones can be put into public ownership via public land-management trusts and thus reserved to do their most energetic work in natural activities: absorbing rainfall, acting as natural buffers for intensively developed areas nearby, enhancing the survival value of the total landscape (fig. 137).

I WRITE these notes while sitting in a downtown Howard Johnson's motel parking lot, screened from street traffic by eye-level shrubs and parked cars (fig. 138). I am surrounded by depopulated and only partially re-occupied territory, the impact zone of a highway interchange. I recall the old Haymarket which once stood here, the early Jewish, and later black, tenements, the sidewalk vegetable stands which I described in 1958 in *The Exploding Metropolis*.[1] All have been evicted, gone.

All around me now are mobile strangers, streams of traffic, wide asphalted flats, and new buildings. Each is set in its own block amid a sea of cars; each is bordered by a new geometry of territoriality: curbings, low walls, planter beds, hedges, and green corners.

None of this can be dismissed as mere beautification, since it is the result of struggles and compromises between the motel builders and civic authority; it tells who won how much from whom. Pubic-hair greenery—those triangular, fuzzy green mounds at the corners, the clipped hedges, sparse trees, low-maintenance ground cover—dictated by an amenity clause in the city's urban-renewal plan, as translated by a cost accountant, reveals that this is "turf," a special combination of civic and private territories.

Turf is landscape spelled out; it says who goes where, who belongs, and who does not; it is admonitory and administered. Turfing messages are writ large across cities in new property lines and identified boundaries; on maps and in documents; with hedges, fences, walls, curbs; by

Turf

138. *Scraggly planting in foreground, small green plantings in middle distance come from regulations. This is a variety of civic turf, declared in renewal regulations. View from motel parking lot in downtown Louisville, Kentucky.*

139, 140. *Lafayette Square, an old residential enclave in St. Louis, began attracting newcomers and restorers in 1960's, and is now a focus of city-aided turfing activities.*

139

LAFAYETTE SQUARE
RESTORATION PLAN
ST. LOUIS CITY PLAN COMMISSION   FALL 1971

LEGEND

RESTORED STRUCTURE
NEW STRUCTURE
NEIGHBORHOOD BOUNDARY
PROPOSED ENTRANCES

SCALE IN FEET
0'   100'   200'   400'   600'

means of signs, symbols, markers, locks, directions, and warnings; and beyond all this, in human images and attitudes. The entire American landscape is being partitioned—faster and in greater detail than ever before—into turf. I am using turf to indicate territorial space that is used or occupied, either principally or exclusively, by one identity group and thus made inaccessible to others.

The carving up of American landscape into turf has been under way for a long time. Setting up private streets and estates, exclusive suburbs, and other apparatus of hauteur is old stuff in America, and long the butt of democratic jokes and scorn. In the 1890's, in St. Louis, the creation of private streets was an upper-status operation. Developers were busy setting up the earliest of forty-seven magnificent private places. All were laid out by a remarkable surveyor named Julius Pitzman; all were gated, lined with imposing mansions, and the objects of envy and civic pride.[2]

In the 1960's there began a new boom in private place-making in St. Louis (figs. 139 and 140), but no longer was it a device of the top elite. Scores of middle-income groups are now getting together to create private streets out of what once were totally public streets (fig. 141).[3] The legal process takes twelve to twenty-four months.

Once an upper-class diversion, turfing has become a middle-class preoccupation. It is widely practiced in slum neighborhoods, and, in view of the concentration of burglary and thievery in the poorest districts, this should be no surprise. Turfing thus knows no class barriers. It is a kind of creeping exclusionism that has moved quickly down the class ladder (fig. 142). It cuts through society from top to bottom—from the slums of South Chicago, where the Mighty Blackstone Rangers were spray-painting their slogans on neighborhood walls in the 1960's, to the Denver suburb of Cherry Hills Village, whose country club members enjoy the protection of thirteen landscape screening devices to separate their clubhouse from the passing public on West Quincy Avenue to the south: irrigation ditch, steep bank, chain-link fence, barbed wire, sign, hedgerow, kiosk, island, lake, golf fairway, sand trap, base planting around the clubhouse, plus the overall distance of some 1,500 feet.

141. Mass production of turf: how-to-do-it books on city planning are full of instructions on turfing by other names.

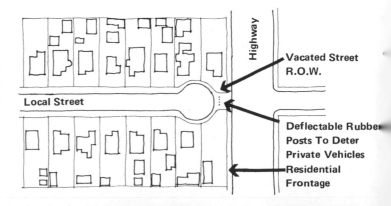

142. *Turf-it-yourself signs like this are provided at truck stops to set up a restricted eating zone inside restaurant near junction of Interstate 10 and Florida 301.*

Turfing from Small Beginnings

We learn early those personal tactics and long-term strategies that help us in staking out claims on territory (fig. 143). Such small beginnings are echoed on the larger landscape. Let us watch closely while a family of five shows us their strategy: father, mother, and three children of 7, 10, and 14. They are moving into the huge waiting room of the San Juan air terminal; it is the annual spring holiday rush into and out of Puerto Rico. Observe the sequence of events as they stake out territorial claims to a large space at the back of the room to wait for Pop. First, down go the bags in a U-shaped corral on the floor, with the open end toward Pop. Mom latches onto an unattended wheelchair and stations it as a flanking bastion with the youngest child seated in it. Passersby swing out wider to stay clear of an occupied seat; they swing wider still to miss steel chairs and leg-swinging kids. The wheelchair acts as its own "Keep Away" sign.

Such expansionist territorial gambits work with endless variations. During ski season, skis and ski poles are effective barriers; vacationers with two pairs of skis can declare a turf of 100 square feet in the time it takes to set them down akimbo. Other settlers use noise, jerky gestures, and constant eye-head-body movement as forms of turf declaration. They set up little commotions that signal "Us Not You" to all others within eye contact or earshot.

143. *Typical self-protection defenses set up by traveler at airport: choosing a corner location with massive sand-filled ashtray as a bastion and personal baggage guarding the flanks.*

Temporary Turf: The Fine Art of Beach Squatting

Few places offer better vantages for observing the complexities of new and old forms of turfing activities than beaches—Atlantic, Pacific, Gulf, and Great Lakes. Rights to occupy and use beaches are being redefined in every coastal state, city, and town as one quickly sees in the rash of "Do's" and "Don't's" being posted (figs. 144 and 145). When the town of Greenwich, Connecticut, vowed in 1971 to go "all the way to the Supreme Court" to keep its beaches closed to nonresidents, it was asserting a familiar territorial imperative.[4] Even the city commissioners of Fort Lauderdale, the Florida city whose beaches had been taken over every spring since the .1950's by swarms of holidaying collegians, voted in the fall of 1972 to abolish tourism promotion[5] and reduce the outsider influx.

Possession is nine-tenths of the law, at least during daylight, since many public beaches are closing down at night to prevent long-term squatting and overnight camping. Once vehicles are allowed on a public beach, they become instruments for declaring turf. You will observe that families use their cars, trailers, or surfboards as buffers, stationing them to confront incoming traffic or other threats. If they cannnot bring a car, they will haul in lounge chairs, pallets, picnic gear, windbreaks, and flotsam and jetsam.

144. *"In a soft economy, the only safe investment is in a company manufacturing 'No Trespassing' signs," observed Calvin Trillin in* The New Yorker *(November, 1972). However, along Cape Cod local governments are deep in the keep-out business.*

145. *"I will shoot anyone stealing these lobsters" proclaims owner of this marsh-front site on Cape Cod. Such threats are more common since the Cape became overrun with summer tourists.*

No material escapes the turf builders, and beach sand being readily at hand is the most familiar. Along the beaches of west Holland, German tourists are famous (and infamous locally, where memories of the Nazi occupation linger) for digging their own private little sandpits to keep off wind and strangers. The American writer Anthony Bailey discovered them putting up German flags and "Besetzt" signs, "which means, of all things, 'occupied.' They then lie in these pits and bake like corpulent lobsters, returning to the same spot daily throughout their vacation, treating the pit as their private property."[6]

Whole beaches become turf for certain activities. Sectors of Coney Island have been appropriated via repeated possession by different groups: the athletes have one beach for their muscular exhibitions; airline hostesses and pilots another, homosexuals another.

146. Setting up the signals far from their own turf, resort owners and tourist caterers on Hilton Head Island let incomers know they have things well-coordinated—down to sign shape, location, and color.

147. *Turf within turf: Bassett Hall in Williamsburg, Virginia, a Rockefeller family residence with private entrance and "No Parking 8 A.M. to 6 P.M." sign on Francis Street. Williamsburg's restoration was funded by John D. Rockefeller.*

Turf Within Turf Within Turf: The New Resorts

As one turns east off the main coastal highway between Charleston and Savannah, there is an unusual cluster of look-alike signs pointing east: to "Hilton Head Island, Hilton Head Inn, Sea Pines Golf Courses," etc. (fig. 146). The controlled graphics, mile after mile, suggest what lies ahead —special resort turf.

After driving for miles past loosely settled farms, forests, marshes, and then through a tightly administered landscape setting of woodlands, golf courses, second homes, and plush resort hotels, past guards and gates, one may reach an example of ultimate turf: "Baynard Cove Club," a part of the expensive Sea Pines Plantation resort. So desirable is this turf within turf, that a company official brags that one of the little villas which sold originally in the 1960's for around $60,000 was resold in the early 1970's for $108,000. Such is the premium paid for such environments so carefully controlled. (See fig. 147.)

Suburban Turf: Second Stage Territoriality

Now let us move to suburbia to observe the process of staking out a new house lot on what was open farmland.

1. Legal and speculative claim-staking. The first surveyors arrive; measure out the metes and bounds; post zoning notices, clear paths through woods, put up stakes and other evidence to upset neighbors.

2. Developers set up outposts: a contractor's trailer-office, a sales office converted from a mobile home, stacks of sewer pipe, etc., as visible evidence of future construction.

3. First houses built and occupied.

4. Occupation. In countless colorful ways, new homeowners stake out

148. Eco-turfing, using prickly materials, along the Florida east coast, with Spanish bayonets thickly planted to discourage trespassers. Highway A1A, Fernandina Beach.

149. *Incipient prickly turf: the early beginnings of a characteristic form of homeowner's barrier system along residential street in east Phoenix, Arizona.*

claims, put down their own markers on the landscape: possessions laid out in front yard by moving crew; pickup truck, sports car, trail bike, garden tractor, and other symbolic possessions stationed strategically; temporary fences, sod, seed or ground cover, and hedges of yucca, barberry or other prickly vegetational defenses (figs. 148 and 149); outriders go out—sometimes a shed at the rear corner of property, a junkpile at another corner, incinerator elsewhere.

Such constellations of signals set up by the incoming family are immediately read by neighbors. One set conveys "Keep your distance"; another says plainly, "Come in." Spacious grounds in many suburbs indicate that the settlers want privacy. Especially in the newer brick and stone enclaves—exclusive residential subdivisions with gates and gatekeepers being built at the edges of many cities—many signals are pre-

150. *For admission to the charmed Inner Circle Drive, go past gatehouse that says "No admittance." Road Runner Golf Resort, Scottsdale, Arizona. Unoccupied when photographed, 1972.*

planned (fig. 150). In working-class suburbs the rituals are less evident and less formal. Painting one's own name on the R.F.D. mailbox or handcrafting the mailbox support from a welded chain or an old milk can is an easy opener of conversations with passersby. In denser neighborhoods, what happens on the stoop is everybody's business. One observes frequent neighboring, fewer fences between yards, more openings and paths through hedges—pathways kept hard by pets, kids, parents, postman, and paperboy.

Next, let us examine the screening tactics of families north of Baltimore, Maryland, in the Ruxton-Towson area, a high-income suburb with horizons of $50,000-and-up houses.

151

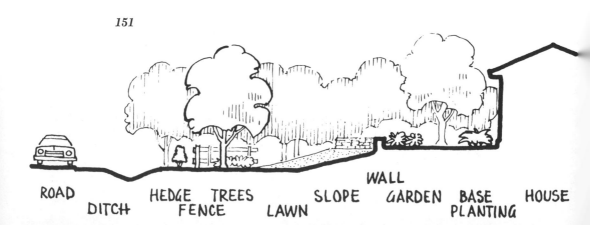

ROAD   HEDGE   TREES   SLOPE   GARDEN   BASE   HOUSE
DITCH   FENCE   LAWN   WALL   PLANTING

First there is the roadside ditch—often dug by the property owner if not provided by the county or town—the deeper the better. Next, a hedge (privet for quick growth, evergreen for the long haul), followed by a fence (English hurdle preferred although expensive), a linear grove or line of trees, and then a carefully clipped lawn sometimes 500 feet wide or wider extending up a slope toward the house. The steeper the slope the better; such elevated topography serves both to discourage strangers and to display the house to distant admirers. At the top of the slope there is a picket fence, a low retaining wall or other signal to mark the beginning of the house, yard, and its formal garden (fig. 151).

At this point you are practically on top of the house. But still another screen intervenes—usually a hedge or base planting of broad-leaf evergreens. Finally, the entrance itself is likely to be tucked out of sight around the side, making visual access from the highway still more difficult. Anyone penetrating these ten, admonitory landscape screens is apt to be either a determined burglar or an invited guest. When I first described this to a knowledgeable Baltimorean, he immediately replied: "You've missed three. The front gate, the big side fence, and the police dog."

Grim humor sometimes creeps into signs, such as one I sighted in the Hollywood hills off Sunset Boulevard:

KEEP OUT
This property patrolled by active dogs
Survivors Will Be Prosecuted

The Hardening Process

Just as in military practice, prospective targets of attack are "hardened" —encased in concrete, buried underground, duplicated, made fail-safe, etc.—so the American urban landscape is undergoing its own special hardening. Known targets—exposed buildings in vulnerable positions on the edge of high-crime districts, for example—are being redesigned by the thousands. This is not simple remodeling. One notes how the remodelings produce new single entrances, bricked-up ground-floor windows, service courtyards surrounded by high fences with remote-controlled gates. "Riot renaissance" is its ironic technical name (fig. 152).

This nationwide phenomenon can be seen in its extreme form in six types of neighborhoods:

1. The central business district. In Topeka, Kansas, it is brilliantly lit at night in colors different from the rest of the city. This emerging enclave is rigidly patrolled by helicopter and prowl-car police, backed up by

152. Sometimes it is called "riot renaissance" architecture, and often justi-
fied in terms of easy maintenance, air-conditioning requirements. Collec-
tively it says, "Keep out, entrance by special permission only." Insurance
company offices, Columbus, Ohio.

153. Supplementing regular ground policing, rooftop spotters with binocu-
lars and walkie-talkie radios keep watch over downtown parking lots to warn
of attempted break-ins. Louisville, Kentucky.

rooftop spotters keeping downtown lots under surveillance for auto break-ins (fig. 153). Merchant police reinforce the regulars, while television monitors scan sensitive areas for shoplifters, rioters, or other targets (figs. 154 and 155).

2. Civic centers. These are on the rise, devoted to so-called civic activities but resembling fortresses as at Rochester, New York, or Springfield, Massachusetts, with single entrances, grand staircases, official parking only, and often a uniformed guard on prowl. Many resemble military bases with self-conscious security measures. The public is clearly kept at bay, and held in varying degrees of architectural contempt—a practice which has spread to other types of buildings (figs. 156 and 157).

3. Large-scale housing projects or buildings, such as the Watergate apartments in Washington, D.C., a giant, tight ship favored by prominent Democrats and Republicans alike, and scene of the notorious bugging attempt to get at Democratic Party secrets in 1972. These often occupy near-downtown urban renewal sites surrounded by onetime slum areas, or else fringe suburban sites where everyone is a newcomer and there are few established friendship or kinship ties. These tend to be fenced, walled, gated, and constantly under electronic and/or human surveillance.

154. Easy to defend, accessible through one entrance, negotiable through one lobby under watchful-eyed guards, the new-style office blocks dominate many downtown districts, turning cold shoulders to neighbors and pedestrians.

THE PROUD
···· AND ISOLATED ····
TOWER

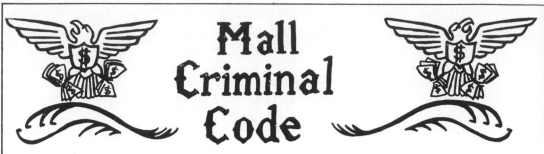

Mall Criminal Code

1. No dogs allowed – even with a leash.

2. No riding of bicycles.

3. No sitting or relaxing on the grass

4. No touching the water – children and adults caught playing in the fountain are subject to immediate arrest.

5. The mall is subject to noise regulation – no loud talking, music, laughter, or any joyful sounds.

6. No blocking pedestrian traffic; keep moving- don't stop to read this or window-shop; stopping allowed only in stores.

All rules enforceable by immediate arrest and a maximum $100.⁰⁰ fine.

The above criminal code has been imposed by our esteemed city council and their string-pulling merchant friends – the Eugene Downtown Association.

This leaflet courtesy of some concerned folks who want everyone to know which freedoms are now forbidden by certain people who think they own our mall.

155. *Leaflet passed out by street people on Eugene, Oregon, Mall in 1971 in protest against city regulations.*

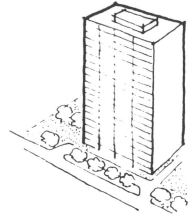

THE SINGLE ENTRANCE
APARTMENT TOWER
156

157. Governmental-federal turf: typical retaining wall around federal building, too high to sit on, with studs, ridges, or other hard edges on top to discourage the public. Cincinnati, Ohio.

158. *Hardened zone: Hudson River bridge between Troy and Albany, New York, has both walkways gated and signed against pedestrians. If you want to cross, buy a car.*

159. *Ideal suburban industrial location: high visibility, a publicly maintained moat or waterway out front, public boulevard for maximum publicity value, and plenty of parking for the daily pilgrims.*

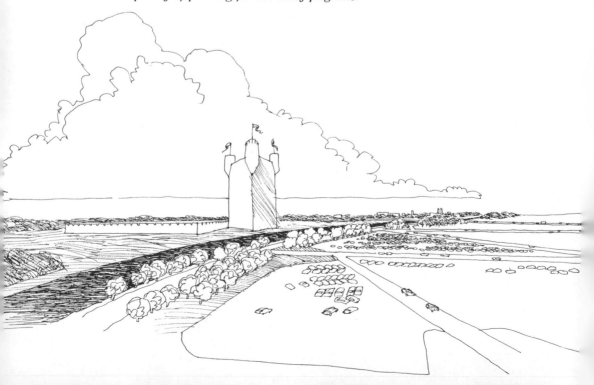

4. Controlled movement zones, such as expressways, bridges (fig. 158), and airports, monopolized by large and often toll-taking public bodies, fenced or walled, unapproachable except by gates, ramps, and vehicles. The expressway system is metered, monitored, and kept under surveillance, sometimes by heavy duty helicopters ready to jerk wrecks off the road. Partly in response to hijacking attempts, airports are increasing security measures. Airports have become outposts of various federal security forces set up to scan, judge, screen, weigh, X-ray, frisk, accost, and detain passengers. They also overcharge them. The *New York Times,* in a national survey, found passengers being overcharged an average of 10 per cent for all commodities bought at big airports in 1972.[7]

160. Dead to the world, military bases such as Adair Air Force Station west of Corvallis, Oregon, appear inactive. But tourists wandering in are immediately accosted by mobile armed sentries and escorted out. Photo, June, 1971.

161. *Prize sites for turf-minded developers have such advantages as unapproachability by water, narrow neck to mainland easily guarded, plus all-around visibility. Arrow points to proposed (1972) site of Watergate apartment project, San Francisco Bay.*

5. Industrial castles. More and more firms now invest in fence-gate-guard-pass combinations that limit access to persons having "legitimate business" on the premises. They perch on dramatic open sites insulated by distance from the rest of the world, often attempting to select their own neighbors (fig. 159).

6. Tourist meccas. Groups of tourists are no longer crowds; they become hordes, and places inundated by these hordes are taking defensive measures—more fences, the abandonment of tourist districts by local residents, etc.

7. Military sites. Anyone who moves about, soon comes to sense that military bases are as security conscious as they were during World War

II, a vast collection of territories beyond the pale, unvisited and hence invisible (fig. 160).

8. Dead ends. Finally, the turfing process puts a premium on dead-end locations, which, by their very isolation, need no hardening. At its present pace, hardening will turn thousands of these sites into isolated turfdoms (fig. 161).

The New Self-Surgery

The fabrication of self—the manufacture, propagation, and marketing of new identities—is becoming a major growth industry, and the North American landscape offers increasingly visible signs of its success. These include

1. An upsurge in the forging of self-conscious identities and identity declarations, all the way from the traditional display by new rich with local variations of the Mercedes-mansion-Matisse displays to the widespread growth of neighborhood vigilante groups or neighborhood protective associations. Observed mostly in older city areas in the 1960's, they

162. Protecting their property with dogs, signs, fences in Gary, Indiana, where safety was no longer taken for granted in 1972.

163. Interpretations: (1) evidence of the breakdown of public morals: you cannot leave your bike untended at Oregon State University. Or (2) normal precautions in a crowded world: take your own front wheel, and lock up what is left. Eugene, Oregon.

had begun spreading to the suburbs in the 1970's. Reporter John Herbers, visiting Houston in late 1972, observed that the rash of civilian patrols there "is part of a wider phenomenon that has been under way for some time—a decreased reliance on public police agencies and the obtaining of private protection against crime."[8]

2. A rise in self-determination among black slum residents who are saying in visible and other ways, "Whitey (or the rest of you) stay out" —a trend giving rise to remarkable wall paintings and other turfing displays of ethnic art.

3. The rise in drug abuse, burglary, street crime, and auto theft, which prompts millions of citizens to invest in fences, firearms, bigger police forces, alarm systems, locks, and an expanding variety of political and territorial exclusiveness (figs. 162 and 163).

Turfing a place by setting up fences, "keep out" signs, etc., may be as much a tactic for reinforcing the selfhood of the local residents as it is a way of repulsing intruders. By selecting one form of house, one color of paint, one style of yard and its upkeep and decor, a distinctive array of fence-mailbox-grass-garage, the owners say as much about "the kind of people we are" as they do about the kind of people they are trying to get away from, or to keep out. Thus turfing is as much message sending as it is fence building.

Above all, turf is a two-edged sword, serving both to keep "them" out, and to keep "us" within. The very act of setting up turf—of building a fence, posting a sign, passing an ordinance, forbidding newcomers to vote, levying a tax on transients—serves to reinforce the separateness of those on the inside. To turf is to apply a special form of surgery to our surroundings, cutting it out of our lives, withholding its information. It constitutes "the martial declaration of the intent to repel all delinquent perception and all illicit communication," as the British architectural writer Robin Evans has observed.[9] Taken cumulatively, it is shrinking our perception, our mental images of the environment, and thus our capacity to deal with it. Not the least of our losses is the ability to know and thus to intervene in worlds beyond the walls.

EVER SINCE North Americans got steam, oil, and then gasoline engines on their side, they have been over-running the landscape, filling it up with anything handy, putting boundaries to it, scattering it with themselves, their works, and tackle. By now, they are accustomed to using cities as devices for distributing surpluses of every sort, an adolescent spree stretched over generations, a way of life become an object of national idolatry. City and countryside alike have become mechanisms for living off capital while calling it income.

Beyond every surplus, it now turns out, lies the prospect of depletion of capital resources; within each boom the possibility of a bust. At long last, in the 1970's many Americans have begun to admit proof of what only a few had felt in their bones: this nation indivisible was not chosen by God in His wisdom to be eternally the most wealthy, wise, and energetic among all nations of the earth. It must learn a different game, play with a smaller set of chips.

Other nations and groups of nations may benefit from our mistakes. It would be satisfying to think this were so, or even possible. But what is the evidence? Caught up in the rush of their own development, swept up by a determination to catch up with higher standards of living, many other nations repeat old North American errors, are captured by the same exploitative attitudes, corporations, and organizations that have squandered the resources of a continent.

Vantages

And now, after such a long-term toot, we face an end to some of our accustomed surpluses. No longer are we to be "People of Plenty" to use David M. Potter's telling book-title.[1] We are becoming a nation of count-the-costers, and it hurts. Until recently we could go anyplace and hang the cost. By mass producing cheap movable goods we could mass produce cheap replaceable places—the same drive-ins, prefab motels, offices, and salesrooms on every road and corner, easy to get to, easy to leave.

But the costs of movement are going up, the subsidies no longer hidden. Our beats and runs, already complex and expensive, grow more so as cheap petroleum reserves dwindle. Gasoline for $2 a gallon at the local pump is not a nightmare but a prospect. For the first time since 1946, the average price of electricity in the United States increased in 1971 from the 1970 price of 1.66 to 1.69 cents per kilowatt hour.[2] The United States supplies less of its own daily oil needs in the 1970's while Middle East oil-rich nations see their surpluses growing more valuable.

Any time it costs more to make our moves, we pause to reconsider; and each pausing point forces us to ask: what and who goes where? And who pays the extras? Whereness, which we took so much for granted as a matter of cheap and easy choices, thus becomes a more dominant aspect of all decisions in daily life, as in international policies. When everything is connected to everything else, what happens when the cost of making connections goes up? Do we shrink our daily urban field, move closer to our jobs? Or do we turn increasingly to movement of information, rather than to movement of persons? And if so, does this not put still more burden on each individual to trust, to develop, firsthand, the evidence of his own senses in order to judge the way his world is being reshaped?

In all this, I assume that many aspects of American-style urbanization will continue to appear elsewhere in the world. Surpluses on which American cities have expanded are no longer exclusive to this continent. Scores of other nations now exploit new discoveries of minerals, natural gas and petroleum, and locational advantages which the United States formerly appeared to monopolize. And they are using their new wealth in ways not unlike those once thought to be notoriously and exclusively North American.

Mobility, for example, has been until recently an American "thing," and the fantastic concentration of automobiles in the United States (more cars registered in California than in South America) would make auto-mobility seem to be an American monopoly. Mobility has been, and remains, a special mode of learning and understanding, of getting with-it, a means of personal advancement, a way of making it. Most Americans were brought up to believe in mobility, to learn from it, and to see their history as an expression of its benefits.

However, aspects of American-style mobility—commuting, suburbaniza-

164. Booming Salzburg, Austria, showing its own version of suburban sprawl. Photo, 1968.

165. Bustling Barcelona, Spain, with high-rise housing penetrating suburban wheat fields, has developed factories far out on the outskirts.

tion, leisure travel, beat expanding—now appear elsewhere wherever surpluses of physical and social energies accumulate (figs. 164 and 165). Most of France shuts up shop and office and goes vacationing the first weekend in August.[3] Famous plazas, from Italy through South America, are overrun by the automobile. European tourism overtaxes the entire ecosystem of the Mediterranean Sea, and Japan's dynamic economy is transforming many parts of oceanic and continental Asia.

Thus we should expect that individuals and societies having access to new surplus energies or wealth—in fuels, raw materials, capital, disposable personal income, manpower, building techniques, organization—will find ways to express and use these resources in some of the activities and shapes now familiar on the American landscape. They also may assume wholly new forms and expressions. Old scenes will be transformed; and this transformation is now a world phenomenon—certainly no longer an American possession.

Meanwhile, we are encouraged to believe that, so complex has the environment become, so large and unpredictable are our cities, that only large, well-staffed, and preferably official research centers can possibly compile the accurate picture, produce the true evaluation of what goes on and what lies ahead. Furthermore, a huge information industry has developed to handle information about us and our environment. It is linked to the new Earth Resources Technology Satellite; it gathers data from infrared air photos, credit bureaus, via Social Security numbers, pooling of police records, and surveillance of every sort. Never was so much about so many managed by so few. Never was the individual's right to privacy so threatened. Never was it more vital to enunciate and to build into custom and law the belief that information about me, my movements, and my place is *mine*.[4]

As all these data accumulate, the power to generalize from it would seem inevitably to fall into the hands of those who manage it. After all, they *know* the score; they assemble the data, own the computers, produce the findings. Their files and tapes contain so much more information than any single person could possibly assemble or grasp. Why not let them decide?

Why indeed! Many of them exhibit a professional knowingness about what is and what is not good for other people. Professor Alan F. Westin of Harvard University's Program on Technology and Society concluded that access to expensive computer systems by government agencies had turned into "a factor in consolidating rather than in redistributing government power," and that access to this new source of power remained so expensive that "the poor, the black, and the students and the antiwar movements cannot harness computers to their causes."[5]

As evidence about the environment accumulates, as data pour into the well-financed centers, it grows more complex and often more abstract.

This is why it must be tested all the more ruthlessly at every stage against ordinary, everyday experience. The gap between the power of experts to manage data and that of the ordinary citizen to have access to it must be narrowed. Expert language, too often manipulated as a professional or official status tool, should not be inserted between changing environments and the public's visual consensus about them.

For we see best what we can describe—not only to ourselves but among ourselves. The word is father to the sight as well as to the thought. Buckminster Fuller has observed that most people never see with their own eyes more than one-millionth of the earth's surface in a lifetime.[6] All the more reason for learning from every waking moment, to force that valuable eyeful to reveal its deepest meanings.

Each moment in this place is possessed briefly, ours to sense as keenly, to explore as fully, to describe as accurately, and to judge as impartially as we can. We may do so by keeping contact, maintaining surveillance, sticking tight to the tangible changing world, describing it with great care, searching for its lessons. Others cannot corrupt the visible for long.

Corruption, wherever it occurs, begins away from the eyes of the crowd and flourishes when insulated from the rude testing-ground of the street. Corruption feeds on monopoly—on the ability of small groups to occupy and manage essential vantage points in the flow of information —data centers, official agencies, large corporate research facilities. Such vantages ought to be exposed to public surveillance and review. It is the public itself, rather than a managerial elite, which ought to have fullest access to the vantages I have described.

The Dynamic View

At the end of this short journey through time and places, one looks back to discover there is no single magic phrase or golden key for unlocking or translating an urban situation to its inhabitants or its visitors. As we have seen, the old fixes served more to freeze our reactions than to free our vision. The perspective tradition enframed the world for us, setting up a package deal from which we are only now beginning to shake loose. The medieval world of low energy supplies, of violent death and famine forced people by the millions into walled, gated, and close-coupled European cities for protection. Turreted and uptight, those little medieval burgs enchant American tourists, but have become cultural straight jackets when applied to the American scene of the twentieth century. We are always in danger of yearning for golden ages that can never be again, for "historic solutions" that do not fit today's modes, moods, and needs.

And so we must develop our own willingness to explore the continuing, unsettling tug of war between what once was and what is yet to be. I recall a moving statement by a British writer that crept into my journals, with no record of its source, describing a current population as "a link between a dead ancestry and an unborn progeny." We must learn for ourselves how to view the contemporary urbanizing landscape—as our best evidence of the past, entrusted to us briefly to be understood as much as possible, and to be transformed by us into a longer-lasting environment for others yet to come.

No placid scene do we see, but one filled with uncertainty, with dynamic action, and often with threats. Barry Commoner has reminded us: "We would be wise to move . . . as though our lives were at stake."[7] Urban life, as we must learn to perceive it and to live it, is a continued search for a precious balance that is always temporary. This is our ultimate and only continuity.

Notes

Introduction

1. George A. Kelly, *A Theory of Personality: The Psychology of Personal Constructs* (New York: W. W. Norton & Company, Inc., 1963; originally published 1955), p. 5.
2. Ibid., pp. 8 ff.

Wordgame

1. Norbert Wiener, *The Human Use of Human Beings* (Garden City, N.Y.: Doubleday & Company, Inc., 1954), p. 134.
2. David Lowenthal and Marquita Riel, "Environmental Structures: Semantic and Experiential Components," *Publications in Environmental Perception,* no. 8 (New York: American Geographical Society, 1972), p. v.
3. Rudolf Arnheim, "Eyes Have They, but They See Not" ("A conversation with Rudolf Arnheim about a generation that has lost touch with its senses," by James R. Petersen), *Psychology Today* (June, 1972), pp. 55 ff.
4. Maurice Merleau-Ponty, "Indirect Language and the Voices of Silence," in *Signs,* trans. Richard C. McCleary (Evanston, Ill.: Northwestern University Press, 1964), p. 43.
5. Michael J. Ellis, "Play: Theories and Research" (Paper delivered at the Third Environmental Design Research Association Conference, Los Angeles, January, 1972), p. 2.
6. Mary Moss, conversation with the author, Louisville, Ky., 1971.
7. Blaine Liner, Manager, Regional Planning Division, Spindletop Research Center, Lexington, Ky., interview, December 2, 1969.
8. Dwight Bolinger, *The Phrasal Verb in English* (Cambridge, Mass.: Harvard University Press, 1971), p. xiii.
9. Ronald Slusarenko, interview with the author, Portland, Ore., June, 1971 (Author's Journal, Book XXXI, p. 153).
10. Bolinger, loc. cit.
11. George Steiner, "The Language Animal," *Encounter* (August, 1969), p 11.

Fixes

1. Marshall McLuhan, *The Medium Is the Massage* (New York: Bantam Books, Inc., 1967), p. 53.
2. Louise Bowen Ballinger, *Perspective* (New York: Van Nostrand Reinhold Company, 1969), p. 17.
3. Paul Shepard, *Man in the Landscape* (New York: Alfred A. Knopf, 1967) p. 124.
4. Camillo Sitte, *City Planning According to Artistic Principles,* trans. G. R. and C. C. Collins (New York: Random House, 1965; originally published 1899).

5. George R. Collins and Christiane Crasemann Collins, *Camillo Sitte and the Birth of Modern City Planning* (New York: Random House, 1965), p. 2.

6. Camillo Sitte, *The Art of Building Cities*, trans. Lt. Charles T. Stewart, U.S.N. (New York: Reinhold Publishing Corporation, 1945), p. 17.

7. Gordon Logie, *The Urban Scene* (London: Faber and Faber Limited, 1954), p. 11.

8. Gordon Cullen, *Townscape* (London: Architectural Press, 1961); *The Architectural Review* (London).

9. Fran P. Hosken, *The Language of Cities* (New York: Macmillan Company, 1968).

10. Lawrence Halprin, *Cities* (New York: Reinhold Publishing Corporation, 1963).

11. Lawrence Halprin, *RSVP Cycles* (New York: Reinhold Publishing Corporation, 1970).

12. Albert C. Eycleshymer and Daniel M. Schoemaker, *A Cross-Section Anatomy* (New York: Appleton-Century-Crofts, n.d.), Introduction, p. ix.

13. Patrick Geddes, *Cities in Evolution*, ed. Outlook Tower Association, Edinburgh, and Association for Planning and Regional Reconstruction, London (New York: Oxford University Press, 1950), pp. 164, 165.

Epitome Districts

1. Graduate students at the Medill School of Journalism of Northwestern University; see Acknowledgments.

2. Robert W. Wells, "The Great Bridge War," in *This Is Milwaukee* (Garden City, N.Y.: Doubleday & Company, Inc., 1970), pp. 47–53.

3. Macon, Ga., Planning Commission staff, interviews with the author, March 8, 1972.

4. Edmund N. Bacon, *Design of Cities* (New York: Viking Press, 1967), pp. 117–123.

5. *Webster's Third New International Dictionary*, s.v. "venturi."

6. Grady Clay, "Magnets, Generators, Feeders," *American Institute of Architects Journal* (March, 1961), pp. 41–44.

7. [Michael Wolff and Nilo Lindgren, senior eds.], "Search for a Holography Market," *Innovation*, vol. 7 (1969), pp. 16–27.

8. Victor Gruen et al., *A Greater Fort Worth Tomorrow* (Greater Fort Worth Planning Committee, 1956).

9. Victor Gruen, *The Heart of Our Cities* (New York: Simon and Schuster, 1964), pp. 214, 225, 331–336.

10. Richard Saul Wurman, *Making the City Observable* (Minneapolis: Walker Art Center and Cambridge, Mass.: Massachusetts Institute of Technology Press, 1971).

11. Bogdan Bogdanovic, "Town and Town Mythology" (paper delivered at the International Congress of the International Federation for Housing and Planning, Belgrade, Yugoslavia, June, 1971) (Housing and Planning Conference Papers, IFHP, The Hague, The Netherlands, 1971), p. 19.

12. Sister Annette Buttimer, "Social Space and the Planning of Residential Areas," preliminary draft, mimeographed, of paper later published in *Environment and Behavior* (June, 1972), pp. 31–32, 36. (Originally published Worcester, Mass.: Clark University, 1972.)

Fronts

1. *Webster's Third New International Dictionary*, s.v. "front."
2. *Report of the President's Task Force on Suburban Problems* (1968), Summary Volume, p. 14. This task force, of which the author was a member, was established October 11, 1967, under chairmanship of Charles M. Haar, then Assistant Secretary for Metropolitan Development of the U.S. Department of Housing and Urban Development. It transmitted a seven-volume report to President Lyndon B. Johnson, December 2, 1968. In early 1969, I received from the White House a set stamped "Administratively Confidential." Summaries of our report were apparently leaked to newspapers during the 1968 Presidential campaign, and one of our major recommendations for an Urban Development Bank ("Urbank") surfaced in the campaign speeches of Vice President Hubert Humphrey. The report was printed and given some distribution by the White House. However, so far as I can tell, it was never published in the usual sense of that word, and now lurks in a few private collections and public libraries.
3. Charles A. Reich, *The Greening of America* (New York: Random House, 1970).
4. *Frontier and Section: Selected Essays of Frederick Jackson Turner* (Englewood Cliffs, N.J.: Prentice-Hall, Inc., 1961), p. 37.
5. Ibid.
6. For a detailed account of the Twin Cities' struggle over this route, see Alan A. Altshuler, *The City Planning Process* (Ithaca, N.Y.: Cornell University Press, 1965).
7. Charles William Brubaker, interview with the author, Chicago, Ill., October, 1972.
8. J. C. Belin, President of St. Joe Paper Company, Port St. Joe, Fla., letter to author, December 13, 1972.
9. Constantinos A. Doxiadis, "Man and His Settlements" (discussion during the Delos Symposium, the Aegean Sea, July, 1968); idem, *Emergence and Growth of an Urban Region* (Detroit: Detroit Edison Company, 1966), vols. 1, 2.

Strips

1. "The Strip Highway Project," conducted by students and faculty at the School of Architecture, University of Tennessee, Knoxville, 1969.
2. Conversation with the author, Norman, Okla., October 30, 1970.
3. Christopher Tunnard, *The City of Man*, 2d ed. (New York: Charles Scribner's Sons, 1970), p. 68.
4. Daniel Francis Cahill, Jr., "The Fast Food Franchiser in the Strip Development, A Businessman's Attitude Toward Land Use" (Master's thesis, University of Rhode Island, 1972), p. 67.

Beats

1. U.S. Bureau of Public Roads, "Total and Average Travel by U.S. Motor Vehicles, 1935–1969" (table).
2. U.S. Bureau of the Census, *The Statistical Abstract of the United States*, 93d ed. (1972), pp. 536, 549.
3. American Express Company, *The Europe Book* (1971), pp. 30, 32, 38.

4. Jane Jacobs, *The Death and Life of Great American Cities* (New York: Random House, Inc., 1961), pp. 50 ff.

5. Edmund N. Bacon, *Design of Cities* (New York: Viking Press, 1967), p. 240.

6. *Report of the President's Task Force on Suburban Problems* (1968), Summary Volume, p. 14.

7. Carolyn Erlicher and Grid Toland, "Elite Neighborhoods" (manuscript, "Recognition Manual for Chicago," Medill School of Journalism, Northwestern University, 1966), p. 6.

8. William L. C. Wheaton, observation to the author during meeting of American Society of Planning Officials, Chicago, February 10, 1972.

9. June Cleo and Hank Mesouf, *Florida: Polluted Paradise* (Philadelphia: Chilton Books, 1964), p. 148.

10. Howard T. Odum, *Environment, Power, and Society* (New York: Wiley-Interscience, 1971), p. 77.

11. Jerry McCoy, remark made at Third Environmental Design Research Association Conference, Los Angeles, January, 1972.

12. Frank B. Stanton, Vice-Chairman of the Board of Columbia Broadcasting System, discussion with the author, May 24, 1972, during dinner for Visiting Committee, Graduate School of Design, Harvard University, at the home of its Dean, Maurice Kilbridge, Lexington, Mass.

13. Richard Wilkinson, "The Georgia Coast" (draft, North Carolina State University, 1972), pp. 4, 6.

14. Jack Eckstrom, owner of Airport Shuttle Parking, Portland, Ore., interview with the author, December, 1971.

15. Clare A. Gunn, *Vacationscape* (Austin, Tex.: University of Texas, 1972), p. 6.

Stacks

1. *Claremont: Profile of a City* (Claremont, Calif.: League of Women Voters of Claremont, 1970), pp. 5–6.

2. Bessent, Hammack & Associates, Inc., "Amelia Island Environment and Utilities" (Jacksonville, Fla., November, 1970), pp. 1–2.

3. *Sunday Oregonian* (Portland), December 12, 1971.

4. Constantinos A. Doxiadis, comments during Symposium on Problems of Human Densities, the Aegean Sea, 1965 (Author's Journal, Book IV, p. 109).

5. George Crile, "A Tax Assessor Has Many Friends," *Harper's* (October, 1972), p. 109.

6. W. A. Binns, Public Relations Manager, Union Camp Corporation, letter to the author, December 6, 1972.

7. Wilbur R. Thompson, Professor of Economics, Wayne State University, from author's conference notes, the Ohio Valley Assembly, Shakertown, Ky., October 23, 1969.

Sinks

1. Howard T. Odum, *Environment, Power, and Society* (New York: Wiley-Interscience, 1971), p. 13.

Turf

1. Grady Clay, "What Makes a Good Square Good?" in *The Exploding Metropolis*, eds. of *Fortune* (Garden City, N.Y., 1958), p. 166.

2. Robert Vickery, "The Private Places of St. Louis," *Landmarks of St. Louis*, vol. 4, no. 1 (1964), pp. 7–19.

3. Norman Murdoch, Director of Planning and Development, City of St. Louis, Mo., letter to the author, April 26, 1972.

4. *New York Times*, November 3, 1972, p. 2.

5. *New York Times*, October 24, 1972, p. 4.

6. Anthony Bailey, *The Light in Holland* (New York: Alfred A. Knopf, 1970), p. 195.

7. *New York Times*, October 15, 1972, p. 1.

8. *New York Times*, November 5, 1972, p. 1.

9. Robin Evans, "The Rights of Retreat and the Rites of Exclusion," *Architectural Design* (London, June, 1971), p. 337.

Vantages

1. David M. Potter, *People of Plenty* (Chicago: University of Chicago Press, 1954).

2. *Science* (November 17, 1972), p. 704.

3. *New York Times*, August 11, 1972.

4. I am indebted to Dr. Jordan Baruch, whose statement, "Information about me is mine," in *The Computer Utility* (Lexington, Mass.: D. C. Heath & Company, 1969), p. 69, offered the basis for my expansion upon it.

5. Alan F. Westin, "Information Technology and Public Decision-Making," in Harvard University Program on Technology, *Annual Report* (Cambridge, Mass., 1969–70), p. 65.

6. Buckminster Fuller, lecture at Catherine Spalding College, Louisville, Ky., April 12, 1972 (Author's Journal, Book XXXV), pp. 58 ff.

7. Barry Commoner, *The Closing Circle* (New York: Alfred A. Knopf, 1971), p. 231.

Sources of Illustrations

All photographs are by the author, and all sketches by Charles William Brubaker, unless otherwise indicated. The following credits are listed by illustration number.

10–11. Jan Vredeman de Vries, *Perspective*, Dover Publications, New York, 1968 (originally published 1604–5).

12. Camillo Sitte, *The Art of Building Cities*, Reinhold Publishing Corporation, New York, 1945, p. 17.

13. Gordon Cullen, *Townscape*, Architectural Press, London, 1961, p. 214.

16. *Orlando Sentinel*, "Florida Magazine," Orlando, Florida, September 12, 1971.

21. From Norman J. W. Thorower, *Original Survey and Land Subdivision*, Rand McNally, Chicago, 1966.

23. By Professor Thomas Shefelman, University of Texas.

27. U.S. Geological Survey, 1:24,000 scale quadrangle, Hays, Kans.

28. *Central Atlanta Opportunities and Responses*, by Robert M. Leary, director, for Central Area Policy Study Committee, City Hall, Atlanta, December 2, 1971.

30. U.S. Department of Agriculture, Agricultural Stabilization and Conservation Service air photo, July, 1959 (Key: ZJ-4W-94).

38. Victor Gruen Associates, Los Angeles, Calif.; photo, Gordon Summers.

39. Victor Gruen Associates.

40. *Central Atlanta Opportunities and Responses*.

42. By Brian J. L. Berry, Department of Geography, University of Chicago, for the Social Science Research Council, April, 1967.

43. *AIA Guide to Houston*, 1972, by Peter C. Papademetriou, editor, and Deborah Poodry.

51. Landis Aerial Surveys, Phoenix, Ariz.

52. By Professor Richard J. Julin, College of Environmental Design, University of California, Berkeley.

57. By Goodman, reprinted courtesy *Chicago Tribune*, March 8, 1970.

58. By John Huehnergarth, courtesy *Newsweek* magazine, November 15, 1971.

59. From Kenneth Allsop, "Fit to Live In?," *The Future of Britain's Countryside* (Penguin Education: Connections Series). Copyright © Kenneth Allsop, 1970.

60. City of Miami Beach, News-Promotion-Publicity Department.

62. Chamber of Commerce, Dayton, Ohio.

65. From William L. Garrison et al., *Studies of Highway Development and Geographic Change*, University of Washington Press, Seattle, 1959.

66. From *A Program for Older Business Districts*, Mayor's Advisory Committee on Small Business, Newark, N.J., 1970. Report by Candeub, Fleissig and Associates, Newark.

69. U.S. Geological Survey (undated), from Christopher Tunnard, *The City of Man*, Charles Scribner's Sons, New York, 1970, p. 111.

70. U.S. Geological Survey, 1:24,000 scale quadrangle, El Rancho-Pojoaque area, N.M., 1953.

85. City of Onley, Va.

89. Gonstead Clinic of Chiropractic, Mt. Horeb, Wis.; photo, Wollin Studios.

93. City of Norman, Okla.

97. Photo, James F. Brown, Cincinnati, Ohio.

100. "Urban Fringe Freeway Corridor" from *Joint Project Concept: Integrated Transportation Corridors*, by Barton-Aschman Associates, Chicago, Ill., for U.S. Department of Housing and Urban Development, January, 1968.

101. By Windell H. Kilmer, from article by Kilmer and Mark Miller in "The Post-Industrial City" issue of *New Mexico Quarterly*, vol. xxxviii:3, Fall, 1968.

102. From *The Europe Book 1972*, American Express Company, 1971.

107. Trip-tik map, courtesy American Automobile Association, 1972.

108. By Bill Keane, reproduced courtesy of The Register and Tribune Syndicate, Des Moines, Iowa.

112. Courtesy Continental Airlines, via Needham, Harper & Steers Advertising, Inc., Los Angeles, Calif.

113. From Thomas B. Schlesinger, Williamsburg, Va.

114. *Courier-Journal* and *Louisville Times*, December 23, 1963.

117. Buffalo Creek, W. Va., flood map from *Appalachia*, July–August, 1972, by the Appalachian Regional Commission, Washington, D.C.

118. Polk County Planning Department (undated).

120. Lance Brown, New York.

128. From *The Louisville Courier-Journal*, May 30, 1972.

130. From the Charles F. Palmer Collection, Robert W. Woodruff Library, Emory University, Ga.

132. Gruen Associates and Environmental Planning Consultants, Master Development Plan, January, 1971, for Kaiser Aetna–McCormick Ranch, Scottsdale, Ariz.

137. From Professor Richard Wilkinson, Department of Landscape Architecture, North Carolina State University, Raleigh.

139–140. The City Plan Commission, St. Louis, Mo., Fall, 1971.

141. Victor Gruen Associates, *Greater Normandie Neighborhoods: Residential Regeneration Strategies and Programs*, for the City of Los Angeles, July, 1971.

153. Courier-Journal and Louisville Times.

159. By Richard Farley, 86 Arvine Heights, Rochester, N.Y. 14611.

161. From Martin Conrad Associates, San Francisco, Calif.

162. Photo, Bryan Moss, *Courier-Journal* and *Louisville Times*, November 1, 1972.

Index